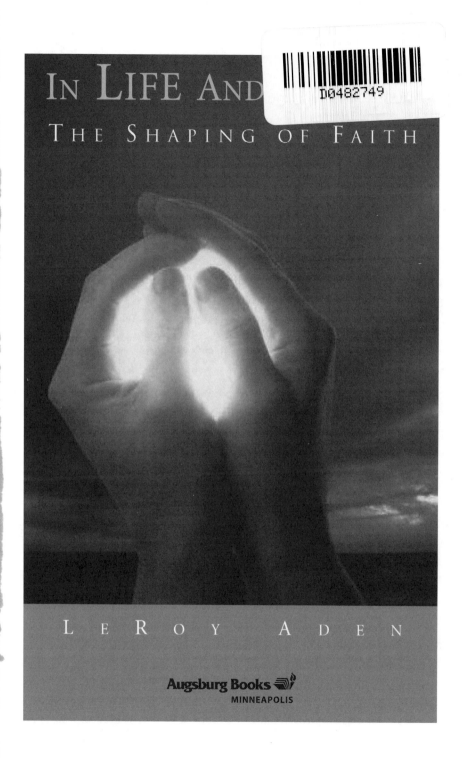

IN LIFE AND
THE SHAPING OF FAITH

LeRoy Aden

Augsburg Books
MINNEAPOLIS

Large-quantity purchases or custom editions of this book are available at a discount from the publisher. For more information, contact the sales department at Augsburg Fortress, Publishers, 1-800-328-4648, or write to: Sales Director, Augsburg Fortress, Publishers, P. O. Box 1209, Minneapolis, MN 55440-1209.

Scripture passages are from the New Revised Standard Version of the Bible, copyright © 1946, 1952, 1971, 1989 by the Division of Christian Education of the National Council of the Churches of Christ in the USA. Used by permission.

Library of Congress Cataloging-in-Publication Data
Aden, LeRoy.
 In life and death: the shaping of faith / LeRoy H. Aden.
    p. cm.
 Includes bibliographical references.
 ISBN 0-8066-5129-6 (alk. paper)
 1. Death—Religious aspects—Christianity. 2. Faith. 3. Christian life.
I. Title.

 BT825.A34 2005
 248.8'66—dc22   2004026931

Cover design by Laurie Ingram
Cover art © Al Francekevich/CORBIS. Used by permission
Book design by Michelle L. N. Cook

The paper used in this publication meets the minimum requirements of American National Standard for Information Sciences—Permanence of Paper for Printed Library Materials, ANSI Z329.48-1984. ∞™

Manufactured in the U.S.A.

09   08   07   06   05   1   2   3   4   5   6   7   8   9   10

CONTENTS

To my wife Ruth and
my children David and Beth

PREFACE

FAITH IS A MATTER OF LIFE AND DEATH. FAITH is the very thing that gives hope to life in the face of death. Faith is a concern of great importance to all of us, if not in times of prosperity then certainly in times of adversity. In spite of its importance, faith is challenged from many different directions in our day. Our this-worldly outlook has settled us into what is tangible and contemporary. The scientific disciplines have convinced us that only empirical methods lead to reliable conclusions. Biblical scholarship has cast doubt on any uncritical reading of Scripture, and the faith of our childhood withers on the vine of a more mature world. If our faith is to serve us at all, or is even to survive, it needs our serious attention and critical reflection.

Faith can be understood in different ways, depending on its religious context, but I will deal with faith from a Christian point of view. From this perspective, faith is both a gift from God and a human response. It is activated by God's grace, but it is also a grasping or holding onto God's grace. I want to focus on the grasping side of faith, on the way in which faith as a human response is lived out and shaped by our experiences. This book will not simply repeat traditional beliefs about faith but will examine the individual's struggle with faith as he or she confronts death.

I have found in my years of teaching pastoral care that the role of faith in the presence of death is often neglected in religious books and even in pastoral books on grief. Those books tend to follow secular psychotherapy in seeing death as a psychological struggle with feelings rather than as a spiritual struggle with faith.

For example, Robert E. Neale's *The Art of Dying*[1] guides readers through a series of exercises that are designed to help them explore this relation to death. It soon becomes apparent that this is another book on the psychological and cultural aspects of death. Death as a struggle of faith is barely mentioned. In its concluding pages, *Counseling the Dying*[2] gives serious attention to faith as a vital factor in the process of dying. It quotes Paul Tillich's definition of faith as a "state of ultimate concern," but by that phrase it means being concerned about one's "own inner development." The book becomes a psychological and philosophical discussion of faith's role at the approach of death, but it is not at all satisfying in terms of a religious, let alone a Christian, understanding of faith. A third book, *The Psychiatrist and the Dying Patient,*[3] describes in detail the therapist's role with a person who is dying, but it, too, is not designed to deal with the patient's faith as it confronts death. Paul Irion, *Hospice and Ministry,*[4] deals with the many facets of hospice care and includes an extended discussion of the role of the pastor as a member of the hospice team, but it hardly touches on the role of faith, even when the index refers the reader to the topic of faith. My hope is that this book will fill a critical need for all who face death and wonder about the role of faith in relation to this defining moment that comes to all.

GROWING FAITH

One of the primary concerns I want to address in this book is the growth of faith in the struggle with death. I want to distinguish my approach to this concern from two famous developmental approaches. The first approach uses a life-cycle theory like Erik E. Erikson's and maintains that faith can and does take different forms depending on the age of the individual. I used this approach in an earlier work[5] and found that the stages of life from infancy to old age faith can take eight different forms, depending on the developmental struggle in which the individual is immersed. In various stages, faith can be primarily trust, courage, obedience, assent, identity, self-surrender, unconditional caring, or unconditional acceptance. The second approach uses a structural theory like James W. Fowler[6] and maintains that faith is determined in part by the cognitive development of the individual. As a person matures, faith may mature as well. According to Fowler, a mature adult's faith tends to transcend the self and be characterized by a quality of universal concern.

Both the life-cycle and the cognitive approaches have made significant contributions to our understanding of faith as a changing or evolving phenomenon. But I want to focus on how faith responds to life-situations, how it is changed and hopefully refined as it struggles with critical incidents in the life of the individual, especially as it struggles with diminished life and death. My observations are not isolated from the contributions of the developmental approaches, for if faith changes and matures it is a product of both developmental and historical factors.

THE AUDIENCE

This book is addressed to a number of different audiences. Primarily, it is addressed to all Christians who wonder what faith has to offer as they face death. It may be especially helpful to those who think that faith ought to provide a ready answer to life's problems. Stories of the marvelous works of faith in adverse circumstances or even funeral sermons that override the mourner's grief by dwelling on the anesthetic effects of faith, can leave us with the impression that if we have enough faith we will experience the joy of dying in Christ rather than the pain of loss. In some cases faith may have that effect, but for most of us loss is real and grief must have its day. Faith neither disarms nor cancels out our grief. This stubborn and undeniable fact in no way reflects on the sincerity or viability of our faith. Instead, faith and grief belong together. They are interrelated parts of the same experience or, to be more specific, faith enables us to grieve even as it is refined by our grief.

The book also addresses pastors, chaplains, and pastoral counselors who believe that by attending to the emotions of grief they have exhausted all the issues or struggles involved in grief. Since the days of Erich Lindemann,[7] pastoral care-givers have helped us to see that ministry must take seriously the mourner's anxiety, guilt, anger, and loneliness in addition to his or her sadness. However valuable this approach may be, it does not fathom the depth of the struggle. Grief is also a struggle of faith, a test of our relationship with God. In this book, I will focus on that struggle and attempt to illuminate its many facets with the hope that those who minister to laypersons in grief will be sensitive to their issues of faith.

LOOKING AHEAD

Chapter 1 sets the stage by dealing with the fundamentals of faith. I start by describing what can be called a simple faith, a faith that consists of certain beliefs about God that are relatively untested by life. The chapter then proceeds to a more sophisticated faith, one that actually comes out of a life-transforming experience. Here I discuss Paul's understanding of faith, which is lifted up as a desirable end-point of our growth in faith, because it gave Paul a profound understanding of God and an unconditional commitment to God's mission. The movement from a simple faith to a more refined faith is not automatic or linear. Instead, elements of both kinds of faith can and do co-exist in any instance of faith, and either one of them can provide comfort to the ardent believer. Nevertheless, my focus is on how faith is tested and hopefully refined in the traumatic moment when we struggle with death.

Chapter 2 describes one of faith's possible reactions when it confronts death, either the death of a loved one or one's own death. It turns faint and fails to give the believer the courage or the comfort that was expected. I examine some of the reasons why faith is fragile, and in the process lift up five characteristics of death that make it a dreaded experience. The dreadfulness of death, in turn, underscores the need for a firm and refined faith. However, given the terror of death we often search for immediate reassurance.

We often try to find that reassurance by taking matters into our own hands. Chapter 3 describes four ways in which we try to console ourselves: We delete death from life, attribute death to the will of God, lose ourselves in the mundane, or strive to achieve immortality. All four ways are instances of the self having faith in itself, and thus all are at best temporary reprieves.

Beginning in chapter 4, I will look at different dimensions of faith. Already chapter 2, with its discussion of the frailty of faith, deals with a dimension of faith, but chapter 4 will turn to its more positive qualities. Chapter 4 discusses the foolishness of faith, the way in which faith defies rational explanation and clings to God in spite of all discouragements. In the process, faith can grow in three significant ways. Finally a greater understanding of the Christian concept of hope is introduced.

In chapter 5, I turn to the tenacity of faith, to the way in which faith remains firm in its commitment. I describe the benefits of a tenacious faith in relation to death's power, isolation, and finality. The chapter ends on a pastoral note by considering petitionary prayer as a practical expression of faith's tenacity.

The assurances of faith are the subject of chapter 6. For Paul, God's threefold relation to the world as Father, Son, and Holy Spirit results in a threefold assurance in the face of death. We have the assurance of God's care, the assurance of God's grace, and the assurance of God's renewal. These benefits become real in the life of the suffering believer only when they are given concrete form in human relationships.

Chapter 7 introduces another dimension of faith, which I call its "fruits." These fruits are not those manifested in the community of believers, but those that are manifested in the self's relation to itself. Faith enables us to accept what was, to live with what is, and to embrace what is to come as we face the final stages of dying. In other words, faith grants us not only peace with God (chapter 6) but also peace with ourselves. To put it in relational terms, by being at peace with God we can also be at peace with ourselves and can celebrate the life that God has given us and the life that God has prepared for us.

The concluding chapter 8 deals with forms of faith, with the way in which faith is manifested in two different persons who are involved in a struggle with death. These "cases" are not offered as models of faith to emulate but as reminders of the harsh reality of the struggle and as instances of the varied response of faith to that reality. I turn first to Martin Luther who lost his thirteen-year-old daughter to death. I then take up a contemporary instance of imminent death and examine the concrete role that faith plays in a time of great tribulation. The chapter ends by describing faith as a leap of trust in moments of darkness and doubt.

CHAPTER 1

THE FUNDAMENTALS OF FAITH

C. S. LEWIS WAS FIFTY-FOUR AND A CONFIRMED bachelor when he met Joy Davidson Gresham in 1952. Two years later Lewis and Joy were married, and four years after that she died of incurable cancer. Lewis was plunged into intense grief, and though he was a renowned Christian apologist his faith was profoundly shaken. He thought he had reckoned with the possibility of loss and suffering, thought he had built up his faith knowing that life promises no permanent happiness, but when Joy's death came his faith fell like a "house of cards." He uses the analogy of a rope to describe his experience: "It is easy to say you believe a rope to be strong and sound as long as you are merely using it to cord a box. But suppose you had to hang by that rope over a precipice. Wouldn't you then first discover how much you really trusted it?"[1]

When Joy died, Lewis found that what he thought was strong and dependable turned out to be a figment of his imagination. Even later when he began to experience a "restoration of faith," he anticipated that it might turn out to be "only one more house of cards."[2] And he is honest enough to confess that he will not know "until the next blow comes" and tests his faith. Lewis' experience shows that faith changes and matures, that the faith that he had at the end was not the faith that he had at the beginning.

Harold S. Kushner records a similar experience. As a rabbi, he tried to "do what was right in the sight of God," and he believed what he had been taught, namely, that God was "an all-wise, all-powerful parent figure who would treat us as our earthly parents did, or even better. If we were obedient and deserving, He would reward us."[3]

Then Rabbi Kushner's son Aaron was diagnosed with a condition called *progeria*, "rapid aging." Eleven years later when Aaron was fourteen, he died, leaving Kushner with a prolonged struggle with God. How could God be just and loving and allow Aaron to live a tortured life? How could God be all-powerful and stand by helplessly as Aaron died? Kushner's faith was found wanting, and through a long process of re-examination he had to revise his understanding of God and the world.

What fascinates us—and troubles us—is that the faith of each of these devout men was shattered when loss and suffering appeared. The next chapter considers why faith is often so fragile in the face of suffering. But before we get there we need to clarify the nature of faith—not what the textbooks say about faith but what faith frequently looks like experientially before it encounters life's trials and tribulations. What are the major beliefs of an unreflective, let alone an untested, faith? What does a simple faith that is relatively untested by life believe about God and the world? It's difficult to draw an all-inclusive picture, but we can get a basic portrait by reflecting on the experience of C. S. Lewis and Harold Kushner, and by reflecting on our own experience.

THE MAKINGS OF A SIMPLE FAITH

We've probably all heard people say, usually in the presence of someone who is laying out the fine points of their belief system, "That's well and good, but I just have a simple faith." We may agree or disagree with them about the value of a simple faith, but we have probably not spent much time thinking about what their faith might look like. Upon further reflection, a simple faith seems to be composed of at least three major beliefs: That God is good, that God will reward those who are good, and that God will grant us fulfillment.

God Is Good

If our parents were believers at all, we were taught from little on up that God is caring and can be trusted. Martin Luther puts it well in his Explanation to the First Article: God "daily provides abundantly for all the needs of my life, protects me from all danger, and guards and keeps me from all evil."[4] Luther's quote indicates that along with the assertion that God is good, we often hold the related belief that life is good. In fact, the one tends to reinforce our understanding of the other.

Sometimes our experience, like C. S. Lewis' experience, does not correspond to this promise. Lewis had an extended struggle with the assumed goodness of God after his wife died. He expresses his pain by saying,

> If God's goodness is inconsistent with hurting us, then either God is not good or there is no God: for in the only life we know He hurts us beyond our worse fears and beyond all we can imagine. . . . What reason have we, except our own desperate wishes, to believe that God is, by any standard we can conceive, 'good'? Doesn't all the prima facie evidence suggest exactly the opposite?[5]

Lewis' torment leads him to describe God at different times as a clown who gives and takes away,[6] as a vivisector who cuts apart,[7] as a Cosmic Sadist who enjoys seeing people suffer.[8]

This torrent against God is Lewis' grief speaking, and we must take his suffering seriously. In the end, though, his experience, like ours, may not cast doubt on the goodness of God as much as it does on our understanding of the goodness of God. Before our lives hit a speed-bump, it is easy to misinterpret God's goodness in one or more ways.

First, we think that God's goodness means that God will save us from suffering and hurt, that our lives will really by-pass the dark valleys. Generally, we hold this belief without being aware of it until some misfortune overtakes us. Then we are taken by surprise and find ourselves doubting the goodness of God, because the course of our life does not correspond with our understanding of God.

Our expectations of God are determined not just by our theology but also by our cultural milieu. In America, we think that life ought to be good and that we should prosper. September 11, 2001, was a blow to this optimism but not a final blow. We mobilized all kinds of forces to hunt down the evil-doers and to try to insure that our freedom, and our good life, remained secure. The evil-doers were harder to extinguish than we thought, but we live with the presidential promise that we will find them and destroy them.

If our temporal leaders can promise to lead us back to the good life, surely God will prevail and provide us with an abundant life. So we go about our business, occasionally looking over our shoulders but generally expecting our good life to continue. While God indeed works to protect us from evil and while it is not God's will that we fall into evil, God never promises us a rose garden, a life free from all suffering.

If things do not work out as we think they should, we have a second belief about the goodness of God that kicks in. We believe that God will be an immediate help in the day of trouble. Surely, divine goodness means that if adversity comes or suffering besets us, God will walk alongside us on the afflicted path and will provide immediate encouragement and relief. C. S. Lewis did not find it so, and Harold Kushner suffered for at least eleven years as his son grew older and degenerated. Meanwhile, we Americans are an impatient lot. We live in a world of instant credit where we can obtain instant gratification of our immediate needs. Surely, God cannot do less. God cannot be less available to us than a "phone call away." To our consternation or confusion, we join Lewis and Kushner in finding that comfort and healing come, if at all, after a long process.

Our belief in the goodness of God really turns out to be a belief in our own specialness. We believe that we deserve special consideration, that God will exempt us from the pitfalls of life. We seldom hold this belief consciously, and if we were to express it in a moment of suffering we might even imbed it in a petition for mercy: "God, we are not sure why we are going through this misfortune, but please be kind and get us through it quickly." If our petition is not granted, we tend to question the goodness of God instead of our own limited understanding of God's goodness. As we will see later, it often takes a struggle with the hardness of life to refine our faith to make it a fuller understanding of, and a grasping onto, the true nature of God's goodness.

God Will Reward Those Who Are Good
This belief is an extension of the former one. It assumes that God is especially good to those who deserve it, to those who are righteous. Of course, the opposite of this belief is that God punishes the wicked. We apply this retributive

understanding of God to our advantage. We identify our-selves as the righteous ones and relegate those whom we do not like to a realm outside God's care. This interpreta-tion works as long as we enjoy prosperity, but sooner or later—often sooner—we hit a sharp bump in the road.

The title of Kushner's book, *When Bad Things Happen to Good People,* foretells a major struggle with God. God did not do what was expected, that is, reward Kushner for trying to do what was right in the sight of God. On the contrary, Kushner's son died. In the ensuing struggle, Kushner examines several ways in which people try to defend and preserve the belief that God rewards those who are good. First, they maintain that while in the short run the wicked may prosper, in the long run the wicked will "wither like the grass" and the righteous will be rewarded.[9] Second, they suggest that God has reasons to do what God does and that we should not question God's wisdom.[10] Third, they believe that suffering, and especially death, comes "to liberate us from a world of pain and to lead us to a better place."[11] Kushner found these explanations, and a few more like them, neither convincing nor comforting as he struggled with Aaron's dying. They simply do not make the belief that God is just and fair any easier to understand or to take.

Nevertheless, Kushner is able to hang onto the belief that God is just and fair by cleansing it of its retributive aspects. He maintains that God does not mete out rewards and pun-ishments on the basis of merit. He pushes his revision of God another step. He gives up on the belief that "God is all-powerful and causes everything that happens in the world."[12] To assert God's powerlessness is startling until we realize that Kushner is not talking about God's absolute power but about God's relative power. God cannot suspend or correct what goes awry in our lives without unwanted consequences. Kushner gives four reasons.

One, if creation is not totally finished, occasionally things will happen that are outside the established order and are independent of God's will. These "quirks" anger and sadden God even as they anger and sadden us, but God cannot protect us from them.[13] Two, the laws of nature are established, and God cannot interrupt the workings of these laws "to protect the righteous from harm."[14] For example, the suspension of the law of gravity in order to save one person from the consequences of a fall, would produce chaos in the rest of the world. Three, God has given us the gift of autonomy and choice, including the "freedom to hurt ourselves and others around us," and "God can't stop us without taking away the freedom that makes us human."[15] Finally, we can become dominated by the negative impact of certain feelings, such as guilt, anger, and jealousy, and it is up to us—not to God—to rework them and to make constructive use of them. In these four ways, God's power is limited by self-imposed restraints, and consequently we are subject to pain and suffering, even to happenings that seem unjust and unfair.

While holding onto the belief that God is just, Kushner has also gotten God on the side of the sufferer. God does not cause our suffering. In fact God does not want us to suffer, but sometimes God is unable to save us from suffering. "If God is a God of justice and not of power, then He can still be on our side when bad things happen to us. . . . [And we can turn to God,] not to be rewarded or punished, but to be strengthened and comforted."[16]

As we have seen, Kushner's belief in a God of rewards and punishments did not hold up under the onslaught of suffering. But that only reinforces our original thought—that faith prior to its refinement in the fire of tribulation—often operates on the assumption that those who are good, by intention if not by deed, will be blessed and even rewarded.

Faith cannot remain in the innocence of this belief and live with the dark side of life.

God Will Grant Us Fulfillment

A simple faith often includes a third belief, namely, that God will grant us a satisfying measure of fulfillment. The psalmist can be interpreted to reinforce this belief: "Trust in the LORD, and do good; so you will live in the land, and enjoy security. Take delight in the LORD, and he will give you the desires of your heart" (Psalm 37:3-4). St. Paul can also be enlisted to support the cause: "We know that all things work together for good for those who love God" (Romans 8:28). Life, and especially death, teaches us otherwise.

C. S. Lewis' developing relationship with Joy was only six years old when it ended abruptly. This event was tragic for a number of reasons. Lewis had lived his life without the intimacy of a marital relationship until he was fifty-four years old. When he found it, it was soon taken from him. Lewis was also not prepared to become a parent, especially the parent of two grieving boys, and yet he was forced to deal with them even as he was dealing with his own grief. God did not grant him fulfillment in the way that his marriage portended. In fact, he had to surmount the torture of grief before he could see a remnant of fulfillment in his life after Joy's demise.

We Americans are preoccupied with fulfillment, partly because we live in a society that assigns a high priority to it and partly because our society puts constant pressure on us to achieve it. Presently, I am going for physical therapy, because I injured my left shoulder and suffer from rotator cuff tendonitis. Recently, when I visited the physician, the doctor indicated that my shoulder was improving and that I should continue physical therapy. I have no trouble with his recommendation, since I do not want to end up with an impaired shoulder. In the process of the conversation, though, the doctor implied that we need to correct and overcome the gradual decline of my seventy-three-year-old shoulder and get it back to full functioning. He implied the same thing when he discovered that old age had contracted some of my hip muscles. When I suggested that the body had a certain wisdom of its own and that maybe it was shutting down to match my age, he launched into a pep-talk about how we should do everything we can to keep our bodies at peak performance. Since I got into trouble with my left shoulder, because I was doing something a seventy-three-year-old man should not be doing, I wondered how much trouble I could get into if I had an aging body that was fully-functioning. I also wondered about the wisdom of arriving at the brink of death with the body of a spring chicken.

I repeat. I do not want my shoulder to be impaired if it can be avoided, but it is quite a different thing to imply that we should defy the gradual slowing down of the body and remain at peak efficiency. The doctor's desire to nullify the effects of aging strikes me as an example of America's denial of degeneration and its obsession with vitality and fulfillment.

A more formal and systematic expression of our point is embodied in Carl R. Rogers' theory of personality.[17] Rogers no longer holds pastoral care and counseling captive like he once did, but he is still representative of a large contingent in our society that celebrates human fulfillment.

According to Rogers, human nature at its core is positive and constructive. Rogers calls this forward-moving thrust the tendency toward actualization. By this phrase, he means that given a proper environment people have an inherent tendency to fulfill themselves, to extend and develop all of their "capacities in ways which serve to maintain or enhance"[18] their total being.

For Rogers, the failure to follow the voice of the actualizing tendency is the tragic event in the life of the individual. The failure means many things, but above all it means the loss of one's destiny, the abandonment of what one should be and become. In our terminology, it means that the individual falls into a life of faulty fulfillment. Rogers maintains that fully-functioning individuals manifest a basic trust in themselves. They tend to do what feels right in the moment and find that their total self-evaluation is a competent and trustworthy guide to contemporary behavior. When faulty decisions are made, fully functioning people are able to trust their second thoughts and to modify their behavior accordingly.

Rogers' preoccupation with self-actualization is not disconcerting to me, since fulfillment is a vital concern to us all. Likewise, his particular understanding of fulfillment is not a final worry, even though he does not seem to elaborate a fulfillment that is distinctively human. To put it crassly, with a little translation his fully functioning concept describes the life of a healthy amoebae as readily as it does the life of a healthy person, since amoebas, too, live fully in their present experiences and trust their organismic reaction to it. What concerns me is Rogers' exclusive preoccupation with fulfillment, his unilateral emphasis on actualization in the face of our radically distorted existence. As a therapist, he is acquainted with the agony and the consequences of faulty fulfillment. He also knows the tenacity with which we hold onto our particular style of life, however distorted, and yet he maintains that fulfillment is what life is all about.

Rogers' position is tenable as long as one holds, or at least emphasizes, an optimistic view of the human condition. It becomes more dubious if one takes seriously the persistent ambiguity and the final impotence of our lives. Then forgiveness, and not fulfillment, might become a prized possession. I will elaborate this point in a later discussion. For now,

I want to underline the high priority that our society, and often our untested faith, puts on fulfillment, not just on the achievement of intermediate goals but on the actualization of life-long dreams. Our innocent faith leads us to believe that God ought to grant our wishes, really our demands, for, after all, God is gracious and is concerned about our dying in peace. Faith, tempered by life, will become more sophisticated and refined than that, or else it will not serve us well in the long run.

To summarize: God is good. After affirming that, we are not above putting demands, or at least expectations, on God. We expect God to give us what we deserve, most of all to give us a chance to fulfill our destiny, what we are meant to be or to do. This simple faith works most of the time in our sedate lives. But when suffering comes, especially when suffering is brought on by death, it is often found wanting, sometimes to the point of becoming a major problem. We need to place alongside this simple faith a more refined one, not because a refined faith serves as a fortress against all assaults but because it is better equipped to offer comfort and hope in the midst of life's struggles.

A DEEPER UNDERSTANDING OF FAITH

There is a radical difference between a simple, we might say a home-grown, faith and a more sophisticated one. The difference begins with the distinction between "I believe that" and "I believe in." "I believe that" is a faith that is composed of a series of propositions, much like the ones we considered in the last section: I believe that God is good; or I believe that God will reward my goodness. In distinction, "I believe in" is not simple recognition but an unqualified trust in, and commitment to, something or somebody. In terms of the Christian faith, it is putting our life in God's hands and believing that whatever happens is the work or will of a gracious and trustworthy God. It transcends our immediate circumstances and looks beyond our own resources to rest in the presence and promises of God. "I believe in" is an entree into a deeper faith.

There are many ways to understand faith from a Christian point of view, and most of them have much to teach us, but I will focus on a single understanding that is central to my belief system, namely, Paul's understanding of faith.

For Paul, faith is all about how we are related to God and how we get in good standing with God. It stands in sharp contrast to its Pauline antithesis, namely, the law. To be related to God by means of the law is to try to fulfill all the ceremonial and especially the moral demands of God and thereby to earn God's favor. It is the attempt to make it on our own, to be the source of our own righteousness. Actually, since we live in sin, that is, separated from God by unbelief and even rebellion, whatever we do to please God is only a further manifestation of our separation from God.

Faith as a way of relating to God is the exact opposite. Faith is to trust in God, not in ourselves. Faith is being obedient to God's will, not to our own will. Faith accepts God's gift of forgiveness, not attempts to be the source of our own rightness. Faith is living in and through God without canceling ourselves out. Faith is a total way of life that is thoroughly theocentric, or, in other words, it is being the finite and dependent creatures that we are instead of trying to be like God.

Paul's faith draws its power from its object, namely, from God's grace, from God's reconciling and forgiving disposition toward humankind. Grace's power is the power to set us free from the consequences of sin, from the viciousness of bondage, and from the terror of death. We will deal with this empowerment in a later discussion, but for now it is important to acknowledge that faith's fountain is God's salutary work in Christ, and not our own goodness or graciousness.

Faith not only grabs onto and receives God's grace. It also gives expression to God's grace. It is a conduit of love and service to the neighbor in need. Paul clarifies the point when he maintains that faith is, above everything else, obedience. Obedience does not refer to the fulfillment of precepts or commandments. On the contrary, it refers to a new life, a belonging to Christ, a "being in him" totally and unconditionally, so that we live out of him and are bound over to his service. His service is a service of love, and love finds opportunity in the needs of the neighbor. According to Paul, the neighbor's greatest need is to be loved, but in actuality the neighbor may have any number of other needs. The neighbor who is weak in the faith needs to be strengthened. The neighbor who is hungry or thirsty must receive sustenance. The neighbor who is burdened by life needs to be encouraged.

The end-point of our serving is to build up, to edify the individual who is in need, but more broadly it is to build up the whole fellowship. Paul is sensitive to even minor obstacles that might stand in the way of achieving this goal. When writing to the congregation in Rome, he considers the possibility that what a believer eats or drinks may cause a weaker brother or sister to stumble, and he admonishes the members of the congregation to "pursue what makes for peace and for mutual upbringing. Do not, for the sake of food, destroy the work of God" (Romans 14:19-20a).

According to Paul, each believer receives a spiritual gift that enables him or her to contribute to the welfare and growth of the fellowship. "To one is given . . . the utterance of wisdom . . . to another the utterance of knowledge . . . to another gifts of healing . . . to another the working of miracles, to another prophecy," etc. (1 Corinthians 12:8-10).

These "varieties of gifts" are all given "by the same Spirit" and all are to be used for the common good of the whole body of believers.

The benefits of faith as Paul describes faith are two-sided. In a negative vein, faith grants a freedom from the old life. It frees individuals from the feeling of being condemned for what they do or fail to do, because it assures them of God's forgiveness. It frees believers from the feverish attempt to try to justify themselves, because it robes them in Christ's righteousness. It frees them from the endless pursuit of perfection, or even of fulfillment, because it shifts attention away from accomplishments and makes serving others the true path to genuine fulfillment.

In a positive vein, faith grants a freedom to live by the Spirit. Life in the Spirit is free from what Paul calls the works of the flesh, such as idolatry, impurity, and jealousy, and is aglow with fruits of the Spirit like "love, joy, peace, patience, kindness, generosity," and other desirable qualities. Paul is more concrete. He describes what a faith-lived life looks like as he corresponds with specific congregations. Occasionally, he will use himself as an example, though he mocks the attempt by labeling it as boastful. To the Corinthian congregation, he says, "I am speaking as a fool," (2 Corinthians 11:21) and then he engages in a litany of qualifications that make him better by worldly standards than those who would deceive the members of the congregation. "Are they Hebrews? So am I. Are they Israelites? So am I. Are they descendants of Abraham? So am I. Are they ministers of Christ? I am talking like a madman—I am a better one: with far greater labors, far more imprisonments, with countless floggings, and often near death" (2 Corinthians 11:22-23). He adds to the list his many sleepless nights, his hunger and thirst, his being cold and naked (2 Corinthians 11:27), but he ends his litany with the declaration, "If I must boast, I will boast of the things that show my weakness . . . so that the power of Christ may dwell in me . . . for whenever I am weak, then I am strong" (2 Corinthians 11:30, 12:9-10).

Usually, instead of citing his own sacrifices to describe a faith-filled life, Paul discloses his understanding of it by the imperatives that he addresses to the congregations. To the Colossians, he writes,

> As God's chosen ones, holy and beloved, clothe yourselves with compassion, kindness, humility, meekness, and patience. Bear with one another and, if anyone has a complaint against another, forgive each other; just as the Lord has forgiven you, so you also must forgive. Above all, clothe yourselves with love, which binds everything together in perfect harmony. And let the peace of Christ rule in your hearts, to which indeed you were called in the one body. And be thankful. Let the word of Christ dwell in you richly; teach and admonish one another in all wisdom; and with gratitude in your hearts sing psalms, hymns, and spiritual songs to God. And whatever you do, in word or deed, do everything in the name of the Lord Jesus, giving thanks to God the Father through him (Colossians 3:12-17).

Paul's admonition to the Ephesians is a brief summary of life lived by faith. "I therefore, the prisoner in the Lord, beg you to lead a life worthy of the calling to which you have been called, with all humility and gentleness, with patience, bearing with one another in love, making every effort to maintain the unity of the Spirit in the bond of peace" (Ephesians 4:1-3).

There is a giant gap between a simple faith and a Pauline or more refined faith. A simple faith revolves around what we believe about God, and it assumes that we have been good enough, at least by intention, to deserve what God should give us. Paul's faith is thoroughly theocentric. It focuses on who God is and what God does for us and maintains that we are neither righteous nor loving without God's gracious and empowering acceptance of us.

Paul's understanding of faith puts faith out of reach for most of us, not because faith is an esoteric reality that we cannot understand, but because a whole-hearted, unconditional trust in God's gift of undeserved mercy is difficult, if not impossible, for us to obtain. We want to hang on to the sufficiency of our own strivings, at least to the point where we seem to contribute something to our good standing before God. While we may never arrive at a point where we trust completely in God, the move toward it is "a consummation devoutly to be wished."[19] Life itself tends to move us along the path, not by automatic steps but by darkened valleys. We turn now to that difficult journey, seeking to illuminate how the tribulations of life, and especially the ultimate test of death, can test our faith and prompt it to be more mature.

CHAPTER 2

THE FRAILTY OF FAITH

MR. T LAY BACK ON HIS HOSPITAL PILLOW. HE had undergone extensive tests in the last week, and the doctors were in his room. They did not hide the fact that his condition was serious. In fact, underneath their guarded words Mr. T got the undeniable message that he was suffering from a terminal illness. For a while he could not believe what he was hearing, but as he listened more attentively to the sober-faced physicians his worse fears were confirmed.

Now the doctors were gone. His wife was due any minute, but for now he was alone with the "news." His heavy head sank deeply into the pillow. He turned toward the wall and fought back tears.

"How could God permit this?" he asked himself. "I am young—only forty-six—and I have been a faithful church-goer most of my life. Where is God when you really need him?"

In the midst of the question, the fear and anger lifted unexpectedly. He imagined that the doctors had not really implied that he was in critical condition. He raised his head off the pillow and glanced at the cloudless sky outside. As he was enjoying the scene, a menacing cumulous cloud moved across the window and brought back the thought that he was dying. "Are my days really numbered?" he wondered. "No," he answered spontaneously. "I can fight it. I have overcome worse things than this." He tried to add a final reassurance to the thought by telling himself that God would be around to help him, but he couldn't be sure. As he lingered on the doubt, he became aware that his wife was bending over him and asking him how he was. He was too tired to tell her, so he mumbled something about being okay.

In the days that followed Mr. T wavered in his reaction to the news, but one thing was certain: The threat of death was a test of his faith. He had assumed that his faith would stand him in good stead when a major crisis came along, but now he discovered that it was weak and uncertain.

Most of us are like Mr. T. When confronted by death, we often do not find our faith that helpful or reassuring. Instead we are impressed with the frailty of faith. We find ourselves raising questions about God: Why is God doing this to me? Where is God when I need help? How can this tragedy be the will of a gracious God? We are surprised to find ourselves asking these questions but even more surprised to find that we have no firm and reassuring answers to them. Sure, death is an ultimate threat and therefore a real test of our simple faith, but for death to wipe out our faith and render it useless or seemingly irrelevant is more than a little disconcerting. What is going on? Why is faith so fragile?

WHEN FAITH ENCOUNTERS DEATH

As Christians, we have all heard the reassuring promises of God: "But if God so clothes the grass of the field, which is alive today and tomorrow is thrown into the oven, will he not much more clothe you—you of little faith? Therefore do not worry" (Matthew 6:30-31). Or again: "Very truly, I tell you, anyone who hears my word and believes him who sent me has eternal life, and does not come under judgment, but has passed from death to life" (John 5:24). Finally, John 11:25 says: "Jesus said to her, 'I am the resurrection and the life. Those who believe in me, even though they die, will live.'"

These are the promises of God! They assure us that God is on our side, that if we believe in God we will not be devastated by death. Then death comes! Our loved ones die, or we ourselves find out that we are terminally ill. The shock is bad enough if we have lived a long and full life. It is doubly bad if we are dealing with the death of a young person or with a death that comes out of the blue.

Our faith wavers. Suddenly, the goodness, or even the presence, of God is up for grabs. As one student put it: "Since my friend Charlie died, I have been wrestling with the sovereignty of God and with the question of evil. His death has been on my mind almost daily since it happened. It shook my faith to the core, and I have been in a protracted battle with God ever since. It happened five years ago, but still the happy faith songs and cheerful reminders that 'God is in control' seem cruel and farcical."[1]

Death often does that to our faith. It may be especially devastating to a simple faith, but the greater truth is that faith at any stage is subject to doubt. In any case, at the very point that we need faith the most, we find ourselves doubting. Or as C. S. Lewis said, "Go to God when your need is desperate, when all other help is vain, and what do you find? A door slammed in your face, and a sound of bolting and double bolting on the inside. After that, silence. You may as well turn away. . . . Why is He so present a commander in our time of prosperity and so very absent a help in time of trouble?"[2]

Most of us may not struggle with God as intensely as C. S. Lewis did, at least not explicitly, but on some level we wonder about God. We find ourselves questioning God's will or not being sure of God's goodness or not being convinced that God is interested in our pain.

Death is an obvious negation of everything we cherish about life. In this sense, it represents a major blow to our most basic affirmations, including those that we hold about God. But this loss, however deep, does not exhaust the reasons why faith becomes faint before death. There are other important reasons.

First, death induces grief, and grief is an all-consuming experience. It focuses the mind on itself and in a way shuts everything else out. It demands attention on its own terms and will not grant validity to anything outside of itself. Grief, of course, tends to come in waves, but even when it is not on center stage it is in the background, preempting a portion of our attention.

The exclusiveness of grief can be put in terms of Paul Tillich's distinction between environment and world.[3] He says that animals live in an environment, in what is given to them. In contrast, humans live in a world. They build up an understanding of life and construct a network of relationships that give shape and meaning to life. Part of that world, sometimes a major part of it, is constituted by the person who has died. The death of that person means the death of a world. Life as we know it is shattered, and we are blindsided by the loss.

A shattered world grabs the mind and preoccupies, maybe even paralyzes, it. We cannot think of anything else as we struggle with the brokenness. We live in a fog where, ironically, the relevance of our faith may seem very far removed from the pain and preoccupations of our grief.

Second, death undermines ultimate answers. It raises basic questions about life and God. Where is God in all of this? What kind of God would allow this to happen? Why did he or she have to die? What is the meaning of my life now that I do not have him or her anymore? These are central questions, but they are questions not of faith but of doubt. They come out of a shattered world and imply a negative answer. More precisely, they imply the negation of what was once affirmed: That God is good. That life is meaningful. That God will save us from pain and suffering.

Death, then, raises ultimate questions and negates all ultimate answers. In grief, the only way to turn this loss into a seemingly positive thing is to believe that the death is God's will, that my loved one did not die capriciously but that God willed it. While this affirmation is theologically suspect (more about this later), the short-term comfort it offers cannot be denied. If the death, even if it is a premature death, is God's will, it is somehow easier to accept. After all we cannot argue with God, and we may even think that God is gracious in all decisions, so we find solace in the belief that the death was the design of a trustworthy power, and not the judgment of an uncaring sadist.

The short-term benefit of ascribing death to God's will does not stop all questions related to God. Death retains its ability to undermine ultimate answers. It still has a sting and seems to have won the victory. What is often at stake in this struggle is not the realness of God's love but the limitation of God's power. Death seems more powerful than God, for grief assumes that if God were able, surely God would sustain life and not capitulate to death. At other times grief may not be so focused. It can raise any number of questions about God, including the question about whether God is even present in our struggle.

Third, death exposes the weakness, or even the unnaturalness, of our faith. Our faith is often inherently unstable. The first thing we do when we get into trouble or are beset by suffering is to doubt God. This is a temporary reaction to an overwhelming event, but it is also more than that. It is part of our more basic tendency not to put our trust in God in the first place. When Adam and Eve were confronted by temptation, they were easily persuaded to doubt the Word of God. In short, they fell into sin by turning from God and trusting in their own resources. Death plays into this self-perpetuating circle: Sin is separation from God; separation from God is death; and death, given its tendency to undermine our faith, perpetuates or even increases our sin of separation.

Faith does not come easily to us. God must stir up faith in us and empower us to believe. The prospect of death tends to work against this empowerment, since God is often seen as the enemy, or at least as the absent one. Thus even if God is working within us, bidding us to have faith, when we are under the sting of death we often do not believe, but instead doubt.

Faith is especially subject to erosion when it is primarily an agreement to a proposition, that is, when it takes the form of "I believe that." We may believe that God is good or that God will heal me or that I deserve health, protection, or whatever. As we have seen, faith in this sense is more intellectual than it is personal (existential). It is cognitive belief about something rather than being an unqualified commitment to, or trust in, something.

Propositional faith usually carries with it certain expectations or demands. For example, the belief that God is good implies that God will be good to me. Or to affirm that God is just assumes that God will treat me justly. Death shatters this kind of faith. When the expectations are not met, the proposition is shaken or proven false, and faith may become very frail.

We now have a general picture of why faith, especially a simple faith, grows faint at the sight of death. If we take a closer look at the stark reality that is death, it becomes even more understandable why death is often the supreme test of our faith.

THE DREADFULNESS OF DEATH

Death is not only a state but also a "complex symbol, the significance of which will vary from one person to another and from one culture to another."[4] In other words, death may mean many different things to us, ranging from something desirable to something tragic and evil. In actual fact, therefore, there are many different kinds of death. There is a timely death, a significant death, a wished-for death, and a good death. The list is potentially endless, since each person dies his or her own death.

The focus of our concern is on what can be called an unwanted death, that is, on death in those moments when it seems undesirable or untimely. There are a number of reasons why in most cases death comes as an unwelcomed intruder. It has at least five characteristics that make it not just a run-of-the-mill problem but a dreadful possibility.

Death Is Unknowable

It is a truism to say that we cannot know death in any intimate way until we have experienced it, and that once we have experienced it, we cannot come back to report our findings. This truism focuses on death as a moment at the end of life and does not consider that we can and do experience death-like happenings in the course of our daily activity. As Arthur C. McGill points out, if death is seen in a broad sense to mean "all the gradual and recurrent experiences where life is known to be failing,"[5] we do gain important existential knowledge of death.

Illness is a foretaste of death; it is the concrete experience where each of us discovers how our own existence becomes impossible. Every separation from a loved one is a foretaste of death. Each evening, every letting go of the conscious world in sleep is a foretaste of death. . . . Each new period of life we enter represents the loss forever—the death—of that previous period.[6]

In other words, we live with dying.

To experience attenuated forms of dying can serve as a foretaste of death. In fact, we may fear the process of dying more than death itself, but death still remains a mystery, an unknown quantity that cannot be laid bare or domesticated by our minds or emotional resources. It is a stubborn cluster of uncomfortable qualities: It is incomprehensible, uncontrollable, and ineffable. We can anticipate death, but we cannot tame it. So like Tolstoy's Ivan Ilych, we stand before death and cannot fathom it. "In the depths of his heart he knew he was dying, but not only was he not accustomed to the thought, he simply did not and could not grasp it."[7] And later: "He would go to his study, lie down, and again be alone with It; face to face with It. And nothing could be done with It except to look at It and shudder."[8]

Death Is the End of My Existence

The stark reality of death is that it is the end of my existence. I am no more. I disappear as a living, loving, hoping creature. Again, Ivan Ilych gives expression to this threat as he struggles with his own dying: "The syllogism he had learned: 'Caius is a man, men are mortal, therefore Caius is mortal' had always seemed to him correct as applied to Caius, but certainly not as applied to himself. That Caius—man in the abstract—was mortal, was perfectly correct, but he was not

Caius, not an abstract man, but a creature quite, quite separate from all others."[9]

We can keep the personal extinction of death at bay by talking about death in the third person: "John died" or "Mary fell asleep," but when it comes to "I am dying," the unconscious belief that I am immortal is shattered, and I am confronted with the loss of who I am and of what I stand for. This loss goes far beyond the impersonal idea that a member of the human species will perish. Instead it means that life all around me will go on but that I as a distinct and self-conscious center of meaning and activity will cease to exist.

The point can be made in a slightly different way by saying that death is the absence of life. Generally, it is not helpful to define something by its absence, but in the case of death that is precisely the point. Death wipes everything out—my way of feeling, my style of thinking, my mode of relating, my act of being.

Put in terms of the future, death means the end of my destiny, the termination of my future. Having no future means more than just running out of time, more than just coasting to a standstill. It means the loss of everything I cherish—the end of dreams and opportunities, the disappearance of past and present, the loss of identity and growth.

The reaction to death as lost destiny is an experience of grief. Death causes me to reflect on the past, on the time and opportunities that I have been granted. It brings about a critical self-examination in which I ask what I have made of my life, what I have done with what I have been given. I discover many satisfactions, but I also come across many dissatisfactions and regrets. So, the prospect of death becomes a nagging sense of guilt, and lost destiny becomes a penetrating sorrow for a past unfulfilled. In this sense, life can trouble death just as in an earlier day death can cast a shadow on life.

Death as the end of my existence has at least one positive, and maybe necessary, consequence in my life. As a fixed and final boundary, death not only prompts me to prioritize my activities, but it also serves as a criterion for judging the value and significance of many of my endeavors. It prompts me to decide consciously how I will spend my time. To realize that "someday I will die and that that day is drawing closer" is to expose the triviality that is inherent in many of my concerns and aspirations. In this sense, death is a handmaiden to freedom, lifting me above the distractions and temptations of the moment and enabling me to say "No" to things that are not worthy of my time and energy. Aside from this one concession, however, death as the end of life is a dreadful and often an unwelcomed prospect.

Death Is Final and Irreversible

One of the most disturbing aspects of death is its finality. Even if we have gone through anticipatory grief as our loved one has suffered an extended illness, we still are taken aback when our loved one actually dies. We know, in a way that we did not before, that death is irreversible, even as our grief and maybe our regrets send us back in time to try to annul the death.

The finality (irreversibility) of death is reflected in different spheres of our life. On a personal level, it robs us of the chance to complete the incomplete. Andras Angyal[10] maintains that we humans have a basic need to shape our life into some kind of coherent and meaningful whole. We move toward projects, immediate or distant, and strive to accomplish them. When death threatens to short-circuit this endeavor, we may feel a real sense of emptiness, sadness, and even injustice. Of course, death cannot and will not wait until we have completed the incomplete. If it did, we would stall it forever by our incomplete projects: There is always one more thing I want to savor, one more task I want to accomplish, one more time I want to be with my wife and children and friends. We can bargain for more time, but death will not wait until we are ready to go. In this sense, it turns upside down the innocent belief that God will grant us fulfillment.

On a social level, the finality of death puts an end to our relationships. Even as we approach death, it may bring on separation and isolation. To many of us this is death's worst sting. It is not easy not to be there when family and friends gather together. It can be a bitter experience to be cut-off from people around us, not just in death but from the moment that our loved ones discover that we are terminally ill. We become unwanted reminders of mortality in a society that is obsessed with death's denial, and thus we may be pushed into a corner where we are forced to deal with our plight all alone. The push into a corner may not take obvious or articulated forms. It may be expressed in the hurried visits of a loved one or in the detached look in a friend's eye or in the quiet way that visitors signal that they are in a different place than we are. In any case, the isolation of a terminal illness is a stark anticipation of the cut-offness of death. I die alone. Maybe one or two people will accompany me part of the way, but it is up to me to do the dying. I must go into that strange country called death by myself, even while I am in the presence of people who are alive.

In *Death: Interpretations,*[11] Janice Norton, a psychiatrist, tells the story of her work with a dying patient. Norton saw her work as psychiatric treatment, but it was much more than that. It was a personal and deeply caring relationship with a thirty-two-year-old mother of two sons who was dying of metastatic breast cancer. Mrs. B, as Norton calls her, had been abandoned by those who meant the most to her: by her parents who did not want to cry in her presence, by her husband who became very busy at work, by her doctors who could not tolerate the implied defeat, and by her sister who was frightened by the physical and psychological changes that were occurring. Mrs. B experienced a final blow when she became very attached to a Protestant minister who, upon learning of her dependency, withdrew from the relationship "except in a superficial and perfunctory way."[12]

Mrs. B lived in the loneliness of dying, even while the approach of death increased her need for people. Only Norton remained by her side. She increased her visits as Mrs. B's condition deteriorated, seeing her on a daily basis for the last three months. She went with Mrs. B through the valley as the patient dealt with her impending death. As the end drew near, Mrs. B expressed great sorrow that Norton "would not be with her when she died." Norton assumed that Mrs. B was referring to her being physically present at the time of death. She assured Mrs. B that she would try to be present, only to discover that Mrs. B meant that they would not be dying together. The loneliness of death only became more tolerable when Mrs. B decided that Norton too was mortal and would indeed be with her in death, "although not at this time."[13]

Norton's account of Mrs. B's loneliness is touching, but Norton herself experienced profound loneliness. She was alone in Mrs. B's dying, isolated from her colleagues, empathizing with Mrs. B's many losses, and finally saying goodbye to someone she loved.

The prospect of death, of course, can motivate us to take advantage of present relationships. It can help us to cherish the time that we are granted with friends and loved ones. Even as we relate to others and enjoy their company, though, we may be mindful of a distance between us that cannot be completely bridged. In reaching out, then, we may experience a certain foretaste of that final and irrevocable separation that death brings with it.

Death Says Something Scary about Life

Death as the end of my existence, however devastating, does not exhaust the problematic character of death. Death is also dreadful, because it says something negative about life. As St. Paul observed, death is a manifestation of a power that threatens to negate every human possibility. Because it means that all my hopes and dreams cease to exist, it implies that life itself is ultimately meaningless,[14] that the entire creation is subject to futility and decay. Paul says, "The whole creation has been groaning in labor pains until now" (Romans 8:22) and that "creation itself will be set free from its bondage to decay and will obtain the freedom of glory of the children of God" (8:21).

Death is related to life in another way. It symbolizes whatever bedevils us while we live. In other words, the sting of death is related to those things in life that cause us concern. Thus death may be unwanted, not just because it takes us away from life but because it accentuates and makes explicit the problems and anxieties that we have had with life. If so, the truism that death often disturbs and distorts our life must be supplemented by the observation that near death life often disturbs and distorts our dying.

On a personal level, the dread of death may be the threat of lost significance. Death confronts us with the possibility of being forgotten. As we will see, society tends to deny death in a systematic and extensive way. It encourages us to forget those who have died as fast as possible, urging us to get back to our usual daily activity. Contemporary funerals reflect this fact. In my childhood, funerals were an important event in the life of the community and were attended by a large number of people who laid their daily activities aside to pay their last respects to the deceased. Today, rites for the dead are often attended by a small remnant of people. A few may be touched by the loss, someone may even be shattered for a time, but shortly we are expected "to quit feeling sorry for ourselves and to take up life where we left off."

The message is undeniable. The dead are forgotten very soon. When I die, I anticipate that there will be brief moments of remembrance, but the pressure will be on my loved ones to get on with life. I will quickly become of decreasing significance to others. I will linger for a while as a fleeting memory in the lives of those who will also die and be forgotten.

The sting of lost significance may increase my desire to want to be of enduring value, but it also has the effect of bringing me back to reality. It puts me in proper perspective. It reminds me that I am mortal and that I am part of a generational chain of people rather than being an indispensable fulcrum around which life revolves. Our society may overdo it in terms of forgetting those who pass on, but it invites me to be realistic about my significance. Nevertheless, death as lost significance retains its sting. I do not go easily or happily into the anonymity of the grave. And I may not find great comfort in the religious assurance that I am significant to God. After all, I am dealing with my earthly existence, and from that perspective I want to leave some identifiable mark in the sands of time, or at least some lingering memory in the hearts of loved ones.

Death Is an Uncharted Journey

Ivan Ilych was alone and struggling with the possibility that he was dying. He laid on his bed, preoccupied with what lay ahead.

> "I was here and now I'm going there! Where?" A chill came over him, his breathing ceased, and he felt only the throbbing of his heart. "When I am not, what will there be? There will be nothing. Then where shall I be when I am no more? Can this be dying? No, I don't want to!" He

jumped up and tried to light the candle, he felt for it with trembling hands, dropped candle and candlestick on the floor, and fell back on his pillow.[15]

Ivan Ilych's question becomes our question when death stares us in the face. "What happens after death?" Of course, we know the Christian answer to this question, and under ordinary circumstances we may rest in its assurance. But death has a way of forcing us to ask the question again. It shakes our faith enough so that we may be left with a troubling mixture of curiosity and doubt.

Death gives us no answer to the question. And we have no detailed descriptions of the journey after death. There are only general impressions based on faith, on near-death experiences, or on philosophical speculation. Meanwhile, death—our death—still leads us beyond the horizon into what can seem like enemy territory.

We have now described five major characteristics of death. Any one of them can induce anxiety and instill dread. And any one of them, or any combination of them, can challenge our faith, especially if it is what we have called a simple or untested faith. When faith turns faint, it leaves us in a precarious situation.

FACING DEATH WITHOUT GOD

The frailty of faith by itself is not catastrophic, but its consequences for our relationship with God is. In reality, it takes God from us. It detaches us from any promise or hope that there is Someone stronger than death who is waiting for us on the other side. For the Christian, facing death without God can lead to despair, not necessarily a clamorous despair but a quiet hopelessness that casts a dark cloud on the landscape of our remaining days. If we are aware of the despair at all, it is often felt as a sense of meaninglessness where not only our own life seems empty but life in general seems to be a vast void.

Oscar Cullmann[16] gives us a dramatic picture of the terror of death without God. He contrasts the death of Socrates and the death of Christ. He points out how Socrates believed that death was desirable, because it frees the immortal soul from the prison of the body. Thus Socrates sought death as a friend. In sharp contrast Christ, for whom death meant being utterly forsaken by God, struggled with the terror of death. He was not tranquil as he faced the cross but instead trembled at the thought and could not even stand to be left alone by his disciples. As death drew near, he cried in agony, "Why hast thou forsaken me?"[17]

Christ's experience of death without God may anticipate our own agony. Even if we grant that Christ may be more sensitive to the loss than we might be, since he was related to God "as no other man has ever been,"[18] still his reaction foreshadows our response if we have believed in God and have looked to God as a source of help in the day of trouble. The demise of our faith, and with it the increased distance between God and us, robs us of comfort and strength. At the same time, it makes the world itself seem more impersonal, painting it with the hue of unconcern and deception.

Few of us can tolerate the pain for long. That is why we often anesthetize ourselves by being concerned about everything but our impending death. We slip quietly toward death as though we were unaware of it. People around us often reinforce our selective inattention, for they find our situation as traumatic as we do. They may even struggle with their own sense of doubt as they try to gain some sense of where God is in all of this. The frailty of faith, then, creates a breach in our relationship with both God and others. We find it difficult to share our loss. We feel that we should have a strong faith in the face of death, so we end up with a chasm between us. Each of us glances across the gap, trying to hide his or her own concerns from the other even as we try to determine how the other is doing.

The dread of death requires a firm and refined faith to tolerate it. Sometimes, as we have seen, death is so terrifying that it takes our faith from us, at least temporarily. Then we find ourselves facing death without faith, which means that we are facing death without God. Under these circumstances, the demise of our faith may cause us as much pain as the fact of our dying. A cancer patient wipes away the tears from her eyes and tries to hide her bitterness as she says, "I thought my faith was strong and would pull me through a situation like this, but so much for my faith!"

As faith grows fragile, we tend to look either to ourselves or to God for help. Actually, these two options are extreme ends of a single continuum, which means that our actual behavior can range anywhere along the line. We can rely on ourselves, on God, or on a combination of both. In the next two chapters, though, I will treat each option as a separate reaction, keeping in mind that each one often exists alongside the other one. We turn first to our attempt to rely on ourselves.

CHAPTER 3

FAITH IN OURSELVES

BECAUSE DEATH TENDS TO ERODE OUR FAITH—
and to disturb our tranquility—we are eager to find some
relief from its presence and pain. We engage in a serious,
though often an unconscious, attempt to mitigate the pain
of death. In this chapter, we consider the ways in which we
seek comfort or reassurance on our own terms. This attempt
is not new. It belongs to our original tendency to turn from
God and to rely on ourselves.

THE SEARCH FOR REASSURANCE

In the face of death, the search for reassurance takes many
forms. Often the search leads to denial or to a hope of escape.
What follows is a description of four attempts to mitigate the
reality of death through misplaced faith in self.

Deleting Death from Life

The obvious way to get relief from the harsh reality of death
is to eliminate it from the mainstream of life. We simply

deny its existence. We do not allow death as a fact of life to enter our conscious awareness, either as a personal plight or as a social reality.

Denial is usually object specific. It is a personal reaction to a particular threat. In terms of death, it is a holistic response that ranges from the "reasonable" belief that "everything will be all right" to the unreasonable insistence that mortality should never be acknowledged. Denial is how most of us deal with death, in particular the death of a loved one and certainly our own death.

We are not alone. We live in a death-denying culture. People who die are said to have fallen asleep. Terminally ill people are taken from the mainstream of life and put in communities or homes where we have little contact with them. And certainly TV adds to the denial. It depicts heroic men and women who can withstand the most outlandish instances of violence without really being touched by them. And if that is not enough, our nightly news coverage focuses on destructive crimes to the point where we can become immune to the reality of death.

Sigmund Freud maintained "that at bottom no one believes in his [or her] own death or, to put the same thing in another way, that in his unconscious, every one of us is convinced of his own immortality."[1] We will say more about our search for immortality later, but for now we need to recognize that it is a part of our denial of death. Ernest Becker[2] offers a classic study of this phenomenon. He maintains that we humans are paradoxical creatures who have a fear of both life and death. We are threatened by the awesomeness and the possibilities of life and have to filter out much of its glory to live with some semblance of security. We are also threatened by the destructiveness and finality of death and have to deny our creatureliness in order to diminish its terror. We end up striving for the heroic, wanting to be "of primary value, of cosmic specialness, of ultimate use-fulness to creation, of unshakable meaning."[3] In a word, we strive to be immortal, not only in our own individual ways but also in and through our culture's "immortality symbols" like money, power, and status.

Freud and Becker indicate how we react to the terror of death. We deny it and live with the unconscious illusion that death will not "get" us. We do everything in our power to avoid the monster called death, and in this way we rescue our fragile faith from a terrifying threat.

While denial is the most blatant way we cancel out the reality of death, Robert Jay Lifton[4] suggests a second pos-sibility. He made an intense study of the survivors of the atomic bomb in Hiroshima and found that while they could not deny the stark and terrifying reality of what they saw, they lived with the terror of death, and the sense of meaningless-ness that followed in its wake, by becoming psychologically numb to it. They became blind or insensitive to its terrifying consequences, mostly by effecting "a kind of compromise" with the tragic side of the bomb by having faith in its power to do good. We do not need to decide between Freud and Lifton, between denial and numbness. Both men could be describing our reaction to death at different times and under different circumstances. What each of them lifts out is the extended struggle that we have with death. Elisabeth Kubler-Ross[5] makes the same point from a different angle when she finds that a dying person goes through five stages: denial, bargaining, anger, depression, and finally acceptance. Later we will deal with her stage theory of dying, but for now it is sufficient to note that the stages indicate the long ordeal (process) that we must go through in order to get close to our own dying.

The denial of death is a negative but a real way to reas-sure ourselves. After all, to rid life of death is an obvious comfort. In actual fact, it can easily overshoot its mark and make us unduly comfortable, that is, unrealistically unaware and unconcerned about the end of life. We become aware of death, then, only when some experience penetrates our armor and we find ourselves face-to-face with a reality that we can no longer deny.

The denial of death may be good for short term reassurance, but in the long run it has certain negative consequences. Douglas John Hall in *God and Human Suffering* helps us to pinpoint those consequences when he talks about the negative effects of repression in relation to suffering.[6]

The first consequence is that we are in no position to accept or to articulate our experiences of death. The point can be made by way of a personal happening. Last night in the midst of a restless sleep, I dreamt that I was about to die. I was standing in a line where people were being put in a special kind of canon and fired into the air. As they emerged from the canon, they became puffy clouds of ethereal material that quickly evaporated into the air. The process seemed painless and rather natural, so I approached the canon with little anxiety.

I woke up from the dream while I was still a safe distance from the canon. As I laid in the dark, I wondered if the dream was telling me of an impending doom. Was I to die soon? On some level did I welcome death, or was I at least open to the possibility? The anxiety began to build, and I got out of bed and found solace in the sure signs of life that were outside my bedroom window.

I do not know the real message of the dream, but my reaction to it is predictable. I could not tolerate the thought of death and took immediate steps to squelch it. I even felt weird for having the dream in the first place, and I certainly do not want to think that death—my own personal death—is a real and pressing issue for me, even though I am in the process of writing and thinking about the subject.

The first consequence of denial also means that I cannot share my experience of death with other people, especially with my wife. My spouse would explain it away quickly or would change the subject as fast as she could, not because she is a very repressed person but because she reflects the societal rule that forbids us to acknowledge and talk about death as a personal possibility. I am left with no chance to deal explicitly with my demise.

The search for comfort through denial has a second consequence. I cannot "enter imaginatively" into the struggle that other people have with dying. I not only cannot acknowledge their struggle with death, but also I am immune to their feelings about it—feelings of fear, loneliness, perplexity, and sadness. This insensitivity means that all of us are locked up with our own dying or, maybe more precisely, with our own denial that we are dying. As soon as death appears on the horizon as an actual, or even as a possible, fact, we find it hard to enter into the scene with any sense of its realness.

On a social level, we have few, if any, places where we can discuss death openly. The last time I taught a class on death and dying, I began by saying that the course gives us permission to talk about death. The students suddenly became aware of the fact that that is part of the reason why they took the course, even though they had not articulated the idea. So while the busy world outside the classroom was blithely unaware of death, we felt free to share and to discuss our personal concerns about death with each other. For a brief time we had broken the silence surrounding our dying.

The denial of death has a third consequence, and it follows as a logical step from the previous two. If death does not exist, either our own or somebody else's, we are in no position to give or to receive comfort. We have come full circle: Our need for reassurance in the face of death prompts us to deny the reality of death, but that very denial means that comfort is not available to us. After all, where there is no death, there is no need for reassurance. There is even no chance to indicate that we need comfort. Ironically, then, life without death becomes a life devoid of comfort, even though in the silence of the night we may encounter death and stand in dire need of reassurance.

Deleting death from life, then, is the first way we try to console ourselves.

Attributing Death to the Will of God

A second way in which we try to gain reassurance against death is to attribute the loss of a loved one to the will of God. This provides a certain measure of immediate comfort, partly because it gives us a logical explanation for why our loved one died and partly because it gives us a reason to accept the death rather than to go through the prolonged agony of struggling with it.

In the long run, however, the will of God is not a good, or even a just, explanation of death. It distorts the nature of God as gracious love and actually leaves the mourner with a God who is on the side of suffering rather than on the side of the sufferer. It also takes us away from the grief work that we have to do. When we incur loss, we need to deal with the loss and to rework family roles and relationships in order to reconstruct a new life. To attribute death immediately to the will of God is to avoid, or at least to minimize, this process. The will of God, then, is a dubious way to find comfort. In fact, there is no lasting reassurance in the idea of a capricious God, even though it may provide us with an immediate explanation for a perplexing and troubling event.

Losing Ourselves in the Mundane

Whenever I face a major task or find myself in front of a formidable challenge, it is easy to get immersed in a flurry of minor activities. My preoccupation with common occurrences provides me with an effective way to avoid larger issues or challenges. I use the same defense against the threat of death. If I can focus on the mundane and can keep my attention there, I am oblivious to the basic issues that life and especially death can raise. The absence of any threat provides me with a definite measure of reassurance.

The flight into the mundane can assume many different forms, depending on the individual who manifests it. All forms, though, have characteristics in common: They are an immersion in the immediate, a living on the surface, a pursuit of instant happiness. They are a systematic endeavor (attempt) to maximize pleasure and to minimize pain, not in the Freudian sense of keeping internal tensions in balance but in the more general sense of expressing the happy, or even the hedonistic, side of life.

The flight into the mundane is not new to our time. It has been described in different ways by different authors: William James talks about the "once-born" person "whose soul is of [a] sky-blue tint, whose affinities are rather with flowers and birds and all enchanting innocencies than with dark human passions."[7] Soren Kierkegaard maintained that there were three stages on the way to authentic personal existence: the aesthetic, the ethical, and the religious.[8] The first one attracts our attention. The aesthetic stage, which Libuse Lukas Miller[9] says could be called the hedonistic stage, describes the person who lives only for enjoyment. Some specific quality, such as beauty, wealth, fame, or health, may be the pathway to enjoyment, but it is the pleasure that that quality yields that is of primary and perennial concern. So instead of encountering life or the self in any profound way, it is the activities of the here-and-now that preoccupy, and therefore distort, the individual's living and dying.

In this day, losing ourselves in the mundane seems to take the concrete form of busyness, of constant motion and activity. Not only are we busy, but we are busy being busy, actively finding things to do and places to go. We find meaning in busyness and emptiness in quietness.[10]

Busyness has its own rewards, but it also has its own pitfalls. First, it creates distance between people. If people are hurrying from one thing to the next, there is little time for genuine encounter. To bring us back in touch with each other, we have interactive TV or, for our kids, we have interactive toys. To give us time to think deep thoughts, we have "think tanks," or to have a chance to spend time together, we go on retreats. Unfortunately, when we get there we often find that the time has been filled with programs, and the moments of leisure have been made into structured ways to relax and get acquainted.

Second, busyness creates a gap inside us. We become separated from our deeper moments, our quiet thoughts, and live on the surface of activity. I remember an old saying from my younger years. My mother would occasionally say to me, "A quiet river runs deep." I'm sure she said that to me in my manic moments when I would not settle down, but be that as it may we have lost the ability to be in touch with ourselves. We find little, if any, time to sit quietly and contemplate the world or reflect on our lives. We are too busy to walk out into the starry night and be both overwhelmed and connected.

Third, busyness creates a distance between us and God. It is said that we modern folks have a spiritual hunger. I would guess that it is our busyness in part that makes us spiritually deprived. And what do we do about it? We get ourselves busy taking courses in spirituality, or we get a spiritual director who, it is hoped, can slow us down enough to help us see the presence of God in our hectic lives.

Busyness as a flight into the mundane is constant movement and activity that on the surface may seem like it is attending to important or even necessary tasks. Underneath, however, is a person who has no time to settle into himself or herself and no time to engage in meaningful interpersonal relationships. More important, it is a flight from the restraints and limitations of life, which if extended to its fullest is a flight from death.

To escape death is to experience comfort, the negative comfort of canceling out a reality that troubles us. In this sense, the flight into the mundane is similar to the denial of death. Both eliminate death as a part of life but in a different way. Denial eliminates death by simply not allowing it to enter conscious awareness. Preoccupation with the mundane eliminates death by focusing our whole attention on the obvious and the immediate. It is, as the word *mundane* itself means, an immersion in the everyday concerns of this world rather than giving attention to spiritual matters. While the means of each maneuver may be different, the end result is the same. In each case, we live on the surface of ourselves as we search for reassurance against the possible presence of death.

Searching for Immortality
A fourth, and more pervasive, way to find comfort takes us on a search for immortality. Robert J. Lifton underscores the importance of this endeavor by describing five ways in which we seek life beyond the grave.[11]

First, we may look to our children or our families to provide us with a sense of immortality. Or we may widen the base and gain a sense of living beyond death by virtue of the fact that we are members of a group or a community or a nation. That we belong to the human race may provide us with the widest and most secure foundation.

This mode of immortality takes concrete form when we ask ourselves: "How will the lives of my loved ones change or be effected when I die? What impact will my death have on them?" As we reflect on this question, we may realize that the younger we are when we die the more our death will have an impact on others. If we are old, the impact may be minimal and the sense of immortality diminished. So, in order to get the maximum benefit from our death, we must die young, which is not exactly what we hope to do.

Second, we can gain a sense of immortality through our works, through what we create or accomplish. When we do not feel especially productive or successful, this source of comfort may not have much appeal, but usually it is an important part of our lives. In our American society, gaining a sense of identity through work has been more important to men than to women though this is changing as more women work full-time for their entire adult life. Still, men have tended to gain importance based on what they accomplished. Meanwhile, many women gained a sense of immortality through their children. Given that more and more women are rewarded for what they accomplish in the work place, they may begin to attach more importance to their vocational accomplishments. In any case, the search for immortality through work and vocation is an enticing path for those of us who live in a work-oriented society.

Third, a sense of immortality can be had by being a part of nature, a part of a world that will survive us. A walk into the starry night may have its humbling effects, but it may also give us a sense of being a part of an awesome and enduring reality. This sense of immortality may be diminished if we live in cities where we are once removed from nature, but then again we can attribute enduring significance to the city and thus gain a sense of immortality by identifying with its super structures and its constant activity.

Fourth, a state of experiential transcendence, a state of ecstasy or rapture, is another avenue to immortality. This state is characterized by a sense of psychic unity and perceptual intensity. It can become so intense that time and death seem to disappear. It can be experienced spontaneously, or we can attempt to induce it by drugs. In either case, we may experience an exuberant sense of being immortal.

Finally, a sense of immortality can be gained by believing in life after death. The Greek idea of the immortality of the soul is one of the more common forms of this belief. It maintains that "an immanent quality in man, a suprapersonal substance residing in him," means that he will outlast his own creaturely state "of being merely one specimen of the species."[12] The Christian belief in the resurrection of the body avoids the idea that a part of who we are is immortal, but we can still use it as a way to transcend the devastation of death. We can comfort ourselves with the thought that we are immortal, because we will be raised from the dead. We need to give more attention to this thought in a later chapter.

Of the five modes of immortality, the form that interests us the most is the Greek idea of the immortality of the soul. The Greeks maintained that we are made up of body and soul and that the body is our lower, mutable nature while the soul is our essential self. When death occurs, they say, the soul does not die but leaves the body, which means that our essential self is not extinguished but only our peripheral, non-essential nature. The sting of death, in fact death in any total sense, is taken away by this belief. "Man is immortal, deathless, because it is only a certain something *in* him, only his body, that is mortal, subject to time, mutable."[13]

Belief in the immortality of the soul can provide comfort for us in at least three ways: First, it assures us that a part of us will live on and not die. It maintains that a part of us—an indestructible part—survives death. Thus death is reduced to a peripheral struggle having to do with our physical existence. Second, it says that the soul is released from its prison and goes immediately to God. The dead person is located in a definite place, a very desirable place. This belief can be extended to imply that the person never goes to hell, that he or she stays with God, because the soul is good and righteous. In any case, the final disposition of the person is delayed until sometime in the distant future. Third, belief in the soul's immortality makes death a welcomed release from the world of travail. This comfort is not unique to the Greek idea, because the same thing can be said of the Christian idea of the resurrection. But immortality of the soul implies that the body is the source of pain and suffering and gets its due, while the soul receives its final reward.

In at least these three ways, belief in the immortality of the soul provides great comfort to those who face death. It may provide more reassurance to the survivors than it does to the person who is in the process of dying. In any case, immortality of the soul and the comfort it provides is deeply embedded in the minds and hopes of many believers. It is a pervasive way in which we try to deny death and to mitigate its pain and terror.

We have now set forth four ways in which we try to reassure ourselves against the threat of death. All four are attempts of the self to take control of life. All are instances of the self having faith in itself. The attempt to delete death from life through denial amounts to faith in the self's ability to shape its destiny by eliminating any reality that it does not find acceptable or controllable. The attempt to assign death to the will of God is faith in the self's ability to fashion God according to our immediate wants or needs, even if the long-term consequence harms our relationship with God. The attempt to lose ourselves in the mundane amounts to faith in the self's ability to hide, and to thrive, in the inconsequential and to be sustained by the temporal. Finally, belief in the immortality of the soul as an escape from the material body can be misplaced if such belief is a denial of our creatureliness. In other words, if immortality is simply faith in our own God-likeness, our faith is misplaced.

All four attempts to mitigate the assault of death are variations of a misplaced faith. All of them either distort God's image in us by pretending that we are more or less than we really are, or they distort God's meaning for us by imagining that we do not need God. In either case, the need to be reassured is left unanswered, and, prompted by the Spirit, we may turn to God.

CHAPTER 4

THE FOOLISHNESS OF FAITH

IN CHAPTER 2, WE DEALT WITH THE FRAILTY OF faith in the face of death. We saw that faith is often overcome by the prospect of death and does not serve us well when we most need it. In chapter 3, we examined a natural reaction to this situation, namely, the practice of turning toward and relying on ourselves for a solution. Now we must recognize the opposite reaction, the way in which, in spite of all odds, faith clings to its object and gains comfort and sustenance from it. Concretely, we are talking about faith clinging to God even as death tests its frailty. We might say that we are dealing with the folly or foolishness of faith.[1]

One of the more surprising and sometimes troubling lessons that life teaches us is that positive results can come out of negative happenings: Suffering can make us more confident, doubt can lead to commitment, and fear can lead to courage. This paradoxical reversal is also true of faith and death. While death can undermine our faith and expose its frailty, it can also strengthen and increase it. Specifically, it can result in a threefold growth in our faith, especially if we start with a simple faith, but even if our faith is more sophisticated.

First, death can refine our faith so that we find God where we least expect to see a divine presence. Our God is hidden from us, partly because we associate God with the positive, the successful, the fulfilling. We may not even search for God when life is going well, but if we do we would expect to find God in the goodness of life. We may even begin to think that God has forsaken us if we are not living on the sunny side of the mountain.

The struggle with death can lead us to a greater truth. It can show us that God is present on the downhill side of life, that God is a God of suffering who dwells with those who are defeated. We may have experienced this truth already. If we have been shattered or devastated by a major crisis, we may have also experienced the presence and comfort of God. God was there for us when we least expected to be comforted.

Theology gives expression to this truth by using the phrase "the theology of the cross."[2] The phrase stands in opposition to a theology of glory that emphasizes a victorious God, a lofty God who identifies with, or is found among, those who have it made. In distinction, the God of the cross is a God who identifies with the down and out, a God who through Christ appears to be dumb and defeated. The folly of faith is that it clings to this God and sees in him hope and assurance. Christ is our example. As he was about to be defeated by death, he let go and grabbed on: "Father, into your hands I commend my spirit" (Luke 23:46). Faith is foolish enough to trust in this same God, even as we approach the point of death.

The prospect of death, then, can serve a very positive purpose. It can bring us to where Christ is. Like the

Israelites, we tend to assume that death puts us in Sheol, in a dark underworld that is separated from God. As we struggle with death, though, we are often surprised to find that we see God in clearer relief. We find that God is with those who are dying, that God is a comforting presence in the midst of our agony, a presence that is often expressed in and through the unpretentious care of friends or loved ones or fellow sufferers.

Second, death can deepen our faith so we see that God is for us, and not against us. In times of suffering we often experience God as a God of punishment, a God who stands above our situation and who punishes us for what we did or did not do. The Christian faith declares that in Jesus God became incarnate and lived among us. We claim that God is present with us still in the breaking of bread in Holy Communion and with us through the gift of the Holy Spirit. In spite of this affirmation, we are inclined to feel that if we are not doing well, God is angry with us or, even more often, that God is absent and unconcerned.

Death itself can bring us to this point. But death can also bring us to see that God is in the very midst of our suffering, not as a disinterested spectator but as one who is deeply moved and troubled by our situation. We discover that God is for life rather than death and that God does not forsake us in our day of trouble. On the contrary, God is on our side as we struggle with death or, even more comforting, God in Christ has gone before us into death and is waiting for us as a friend and companion at the end of the tunnel.

Third, death can move our faith from "I believe that" to "I believe in." As we saw in chapter 1, death shatters our propositions about God, or at least it forces us to revise our propositional faith. Better still, it invites us to give up our beliefs about God and to relate to God in a deeper, more personal and more immediate way. We stop our speculating about what God is like and about what we can expect from God, and instead we simply lean on God and find life and hope in and through God. It is a matter of casting our cares on God, because we know that he cares for us. In this sense, death drives us to greater trust, urging us to hang onto the promises of God and to live out of those promises.

In these three ways, then, death can have a profound effect on our faith even as our faith "foolishly" grasps onto the comfort of God. Of course, if we maintain that death is the will of God, then we might experience a measure of immediate comfort. But in the long run death as the will of God tends to reflect negatively on God's graciousness. Ironically, the foolishness of faith shows us a better way. It shows us that God is with us in our suffering in spite of all appearances. It assures us that the promises of God will be kept in spite of our present circumstances. We are comforted with a comfort that only God can give. "And remember, I am with you always, to the end of the age" (Matthew 28:20). "I came that they may have life, and have it abundantly" (John 10:10).

While faith is a powerful ally in our struggle with death, we may experience moments, maybe many moments, when we are not sure. We find ourselves asking, "If God is on our side, where is it evident in my life? Where are the footprints of Christ in the process of my dying?" Three mistakes can be made in answering this question. First, we can require empirical proof of God's presence. We can say in effect, "Unless I see hard evidence that God's healing power is at work, I will not believe." Any attempt to make the promise of faith a guaranteed empirical fact can only end in frustration, especially since the concrete manifestation of God's healing presence may not be the evidence that we are looking for. Second, we can go to the other extreme and assume that God's healing lies only in some eschatological future. We do not look for, or expect, divine healing to be available to us in our current situation. And, finally, we can assume that the presence of Christ, God with us, will take away all pain and suffering. We look for immediate and obvious help. Thus if we continue to suffer, surely God is not present at all.

A refined faith finds a correction to these mistaken notions in Paul's understanding of faith.

PAUL'S RESURRECTION FAITH

For Paul, faith at its core was a resurrection faith, a belief that on the third day God raised Jesus from the dead. Paul also believed that in Baptism we are united with Christ in a death like his, and so we will also be united with him in a resurrection like his (Romans 6:4-5). Just as God raised Christ from the dead, so we who are Christ's will also be raised from the dead. Later, we may have occasion to deal more fully with the theological fine points of this belief, but for now we want to elaborate its importance for our lives and our faith.

Resurrection is not a cataclysmic event in our lives but a quiet renewal of life in the midst of suffering and loss. As Cullmann says, "Every healing is a partial resurrection, a partial victory of life against death."[3] Often the resurrection of life takes very inconspicuous forms. It is a relational reality that ministers to us incognito in the gathered congregation when hymns are sung, words are spoken, hugs and tears are interchanged, memories are shared, and food is given. This is to say that in, with, and under the appearance of hopelessness, the hope and promise of the resurrection is present in assorted ways—in the fellowship and faith of the congregation; in the worship of the church, that is, in the reading of Scripture, the saying of prayers, and the proclaiming of the word; and in moments of love and service when needs are met and the broken healed. The renewal of life is there in all kinds of unpretentious times when lay people support and care for each other.

The resurrected life is not just a relational reality. It is also a sacramental gift. We see its power in the comatose patient who when given the bread and wine, becomes conscious long enough to receive the elements. Life shines in the darkness of death, much like it does when a relatively unresponsive Alzheimer's patient comes to life with the singing of a familiar hymn. The sacrament, or the hymn, reaches deeply into a person's history and touches his or her being, infusing it with a ray of renewed life. Even if the renewal lasts for only a brief moment, its short duration does not take away from its realness or its power.

St. Paul anticipated the resurrectional reality of the Lord's Supper when he said, "The bread we break, is it not a sharing in the body of Christ?" (1 Corinthians 10:16) And the Eucharist Prayer describes the bread and the cup as a remembrance of the life that Christ offered for us and as an anticipation of the time when he will come "in power to share with us the great and promised feast."[4]

Under ordinary circumstances we are often not aware of the power of the sacramental meal, but when impending death blocks our way to extended life we appreciate and grasp onto its gift of renewal (life).

The role of Baptism in the renewal of life may be more evident to us, partly because we see it as the beginning of our life in Christ. For Paul, it was a crucial turning point. "Do you not know that all of us who have been baptized into Christ Jesus were baptized into his death?". . . so that we "might walk in newness of life" (Romans 6:3-4). Paul is not talking about a rebirth that happens after death but a reality that begins in our present existence and is completed in the final resurrection.

Faith can easily mislocate the comfort of Baptism. As Victor Paul Furnish[5] reminds us, Baptism itself is not the act that rescues us from the consequences of sin and death. It is what lies behind Baptism or, more correctly, it is what Baptism makes real in our lives, namely, Christ's death and resurrection, that comforts us. Baptism itself is significant only because it is a specific and concrete manifestation of God's action of making us his own and of accepting us as children of God. In other words, Baptism is God's grace and mercy concretized in our lives. Thus when Luther leaned on his Baptism in moments of doubt and suffering, it was not Baptism as an act onto itself that comforted him but Baptism as a reminder of what Christ has done and is doing for him.

The comfort of Baptism, then, is the comfort of God's gracious will toward me. And this comfort is available and real, even if our faith at any one moment is not strong or sure. This is a crucial point in the folly of faith. In adversity, in our struggle with death and dying, our faith may waver, or even turn to doubt, and yet God is there, extending forgiveness and new life. In this sense, faith is not a condition of our being "saved from death and born anew." It is simply a grasping onto, a trusting in and an acceptance of what God has done and is doing for us.

The foolishness of faith does not take away its frailty. In the face of death, we may wonder where God is or even if God really cares. But faith can also work the other side of the street. It can trust in the promises of God and draw strength from them, even though, as Luther says, "hordes of devils fill the land, all threatening to devour us."[6] Faith has this power because it is closely allied with hope.

FAITH AND HOPE

Hope can be used as a verb or a noun. It refers to something we do or have. In a general sense it means that we are confident that such-and-such will happen. More precisely, hope lives in the future, or at least it looks forward to the future with assurance and expectation. Or as C. K. Barrett says, "Hope is confidence (in God) understood with special reference to the future."[7]

If death can refine our faith, it can also refine our hope. It does this by clarifying and correcting hope's object. By threatening our hope with hopelessness, death tests our hope and forces us to consider whether we are looking to someone or something that will not withstand the assaults of death. In other words, hope can take different forms, or faces, depending on the source of its assurance. I can differentiate three different forms—hope as wish or desire; hope as possibility; and hope as confession. Each of these forms has its own particular relation to faith and to our struggle with death, but the third one is a real handmaiden to faith.

Hope As Wish

The first form of hope is expressed by Kubler-Ross when she quotes a patient who is suffering from a malignant skin disease. The patient, a Mr. J, talks about the medical research that is being done on his condition. He dwells on the possibility that a cure may be found. He says, "[I] hope that some morning I'll sit up on the side of the bed and the doctor will be there and he will say, 'I want to give you this shot,' and it will be something like a vaccine or something, and in a few days [the disease] will clear up."[8]

This form of hope always has a particular and desired end in mind and is often expressed as a wish or a desire. It can cover a wide range of personal wishes. For example, "I hope that I will be cured" or "I hope that I will be able to return to my job" or "I hope that I will not suffer." Whatever the specific wish, hope in this sense tends to want our world to return to the way we have known it. At best it is an instance of inertia; at worse it is a form of denial. We either have not caught up to our present circumstances or we cannot acknowledge the possible outcome of our condition.

"I hope that" is closely related to faith in the form of "I believe that," for instance, "I believe that God is good," "I believe that I have lived a good life," or "I believe that the doctors will cure me." Whatever the specific belief, it tends to support my particular hope. For example, the belief that God is good gives me just cause to hope that I will be cured.

As my condition deteriorates, my hope is tested, if not eroded, and I may be forced to retreat to other, less desirable wishes. My hope to be cured may give way to the desire to be able to go home one more time. This process can continue until I am bereft of hope all together. Or as one writer puts it, "A hope that is not firmly grounded ensures disappointment, shame, and disaster."[9] As my hope is being eroded so is my faith, for under the circumstances I may find it difficult to believe in the goodness or care of God.

All of us know one thing about hope as a wish: What we hope for will often not be granted exactly as we wish. And sooner or later, it will not be granted at all, because our mortality will catch up with us and our hope for life as it was will evaporate before our eyes. Hopefully, in this whole process our struggle with death will lead us to a deeper form of hope.

Hope As Possibility

Hope as possibility is introduced best by a clinical example. A woman agrees to a divorce, contrary to her wishes, because her husband is involved with someone else and insists on going his separate way. At first the woman is devastated, but underneath it all she quietly hopes that they will get back together. After months of pain and hoping, the woman begins to notice a gradual change in her outlook. She begins to look at what lies ahead rather than living in the past. In her better moments she even feels that she will make it, that she can rebuild her life and start anew.

The woman is now living in hope as possibility. It is a "hope in spite of" present circumstances. It lives in the future, above and beyond present conditions, so it is not a wish but an anticipation. It does not rest its case on specific demands but is able to see beyond the present moment to an unfolding future. Unlike the first form of hope, hope as possibility takes a certain amount of courage and strength. It has the power to go forward into uncharted waters and to make the most of a changing tide. This form of hope believes that all is not lost, whatever happens. It is hope in a truer sense than "hope as a wish" insofar as it transcends immediate, egocentric desires, and is based on the conviction that life has more to offer than meets the eye. The hospice movement illustrates this level of hope. It helps the patient to live a day at a time, to see possibility in the present by making the most of today.

Hope as possibility is subject to at least two distortions. The first is Robert Schuller's possibility thinking. Schuller is not wrong in emphasizing the possible, but he is naive and simplistic about it. He does not take into account the under-side of life, the powerlessness of our will, and therefore he implies that living in the hope of the possible is a simple matter of doing it. Turning scars into stars is sometimes a difficult, if not an impossible task, especially if the scars are left by the claws of death and dying.

The second distortion is found in stoicism. Stoicism maintains that we should be free from passion and unmoved by emotions like joy or grief. Instead, we should live with a stiff upper lip, submitting without complaint to unavoidable necessity. To hope in the possible is not courage in a stoic sense. It is not a defiant face set against fate, a "taking it on the chin' no matter what. On the contrary, the second form of hope is a real acknowledgment of our plight and a genuine acceptance of its reality but with the vision and the courage to live in the possibilities of the future.

"Hope in spite of" stands against our cultural tendency to deny death in the name of getting rid of the unacceptable. It is hope in spite of anything that diminishes life, including the enemy called death. It looks at mortality in the face and confronts those things in the present that drive toward defeat, because it is fed by a courage that enables us to affirm ourselves in spite of present circumstances.

"Hope in spite of" is usually not a self-induced power. It is a gift given to us, because we are grounded in some power or reality beyond ourselves. If our hope is centered only in ourselves, it is a limited and unstable hope, subject to the changeable nature of our optimism. But if our hope is grounded by faith in God, it draws on God's resources to define what is possible. Even more so, it turns hope as possibility into its most empowering form, namely, hope as confession.

Hope As Confession

The third posture that hope takes is not a wish or a possibility. Instead it is a confession, an act of faith that says, "I hope in" or, more precisely, "I place my hope in." It is a holistic stance that points directly to the source of my confidence: "God is my hope." Or as a famous hymn puts it: "My hope is built on nothing less than Jesus' blood and righteousness."[10]

This form of hope is parallel to "I believe in." In fact, what "I believe in" is the foundation of my hope. So hope in this form becomes a participation in or a living through. It is a going beyond the self and being grounded in God, which is to say that the source of our hope becomes the wellspring of our hoping.

The object of my hope is all important. It makes all the difference in the world. To place one's hope in God is to place one's life and future in God's hands. God's will is my destiny. God's victory is my assurance. What happens to me is hidden in the greater truth that if God lives, I also will live. In this sense, "hope in" transcends illness and death and is a hope in the resurrection, in the recreation of life.

"Hope in" can be distorted in at least two ways. It can be a false facade. It may appear to be genuine and solid, but when we suffer loss and death, our hope in Christ turns out to be shallow, if not non-existent. C. S. Lewis, who was devastated by the loss of his wife, discovered that he did not really believe in the goodness and mercy of God, but instead God seemed like a Cosmic Sadist who was not available when he needed God the most.[11]

Hope as confession can be distorted in a second way. We can easily turn it into a demand or an earned expectation. We think that our faith in God ought to grant us certain assurances, that our trust in God is a claim on divine mercy. In sharp contrast, genuine "hope in" is simply trusting in God and relying on God's mercy, no matter what happens.

Genuine hope has an eschatological future-oriented outlook as much as it has a fix on the present moment. Faith in a resurrection God does not bring new life to pass immediately. Faith lives in hope—the hope of what is to be, the conviction that the old will pass away and the new will come. Hope is patient because it can live with the fact that only at the end of time will we experience complete and lasting fulfillment.

The power of "hope in" can be illustrated by an interaction that I had with a student in counseling. The student was struggling with a difficult problem for nearly an hour when he suddenly came to a decisive, earth-shaking realization. To ease some of his uncomfortableness and at the same time to acknowledge the power of the moment, he said, "Just think! I have arrived at an oceanic insight, and it happened in your office." The student paused a moment and then went on, "I don't know what to do with it." I let him live with that realization for a moment and then said, "Maybe you don't do anything with it. Maybe it does something to you."

To believe in God, to hope in the resurrection, does something to and for us as we confront death. It helps to take away the sting of death by making death not the end of the road but the beginning of a new journey. Even so, most of us will not rush for the starting gate, but when we are there faith in God's power to raise Christ—and us—from the dead, is one of the few things that can disarm the terrible reality of death.

The element of hope in faith gives faith staying power when the present looks bleak and hopeless. Faith as trust may waver and even look very foolish when all of the forces in the present moment prove to be untrustworthy, but hope in a Power beyond suffering, hope in a life that is to come can embolden faith. To the outsider faith looks foolish; to the believer faith is focused on the faithfulness of God and is confident that God will not let us down, no matter what.

A faith that clings foolishly to God in the face of death always surprises and often encourages us. A grandmother who continues to believe while her wasted body drags her toward death is a beacon of light in a dark night. What seems like the foolishness of faith gives way to a resurrection hope, and we who stand by are comforted by the clinging even as we are awed by the tenacity of her faith.

CHAPTER 5

THE TENACITY OF FAITH

AS WE HAVE SEEN, DEATH CAN SWEEP AWAY everything in its path. It can shake our faith and even expose its frailty and folly. Yet there remains a firmness, a way in which faith remains steadfast, or even flourishes, in our darkest hour.

We all know the scenario. A person undergoes great or prolonged suffering. The situation may even seem hopeless. As on-lookers we anticipate that the person's faith will not stand the test, that it will turn against the very source of help that it once clung to. To our surprise the person's faith remains firm and unshaken, enabling him or her to walk through the valley with trust and confidence.

Mrs. K, age seventy-one, is a case in point. She lost her husband to a sudden heart attack shortly after they retired. Their financial affairs were not in good order, forcing Mrs. K to live on a meager income. Soon her eyesight began to fail, and because her eyes became extremely sensitive to light she withdrew from the social world she loved and remained in her darkened home much of the time. She did not complain but made the most of the situation. She relied on her one son and two daughters for sustenance and support. As Mrs. K's needs became more pronounced and her situation more demanding, the daughters, who lived two hours away, began to visit less and less. The son remained more attentive to Mrs. K's needs, but given the pressures at work he became impatient with her and critical of her many demands. Mrs. K struggled with a sense of rejection and abandonment.

Mrs. K's plight could have easily eroded her faith. Instead her faith in the presence and goodness of God never wavered. She did not make a big show of her faith, but in a quiet and confident way she was sure that God was with her and would protect her. When she reached her nineties, she began to talk about going home to Jesus. Her faith remained firm to the end, and she died as confident as she had lived.

Mrs. K's faith had been refined in the fires of life. At twenty-one years of age, she left her family in Germany and sailed to America to nurse an ailing male friend back to health. She succeeded in her mission and married the man she saved. They lived on the Kansas prairie and endured perennial hardships from unforgiving draughts. A sister who had accompanied her to America became alienated from Mrs. K and did not speak to her for the rest of her life. Mrs. K and her husband had one healthy child, and then a year later they stood helplessly by as a second child was consumed by an uncontrolled fever.

Mrs. K could not understand "the workings of God" in her life. She questioned the goodness, and even the love, of God and became so disillusioned that she despaired of life. She was about to cast "everything overboard" when she decided to go into a vacant country church to pray. She did not remember exactly what she said, but suddenly she found herself repeating, "Oh God, I put my life in your hands." An unexplainable peace came over her, and ever since when she felt despair coming on she renewed her trust in God and "leaned on Jesus."

Kubler-Ross offers a second example of faith's firmness when she recounts the story of Dr. G.[1] Dr. G, a practicing dentist, went for an immediate X-ray when he experienced a sharp and unrelenting pain in his abdomen. Surgery was recommended, and Dr. G thought that he "came through the operation in very good shape."[2] Subsequently, a blockage in the bowels was discovered and further surgery was necessary. He did not know at the time, that the first operation revealed extensive metastatic cancer that affected "all the organs of the body with the exception of the liver and the spleen."[3] Dr. G learned how serious his condition really was from his twenty-four-year-old son. He appreciated the honesty.

Dr. G's immediate hope was that medical science would stumble onto a treatment that would help him, but what he really evidenced was a confident trust in the Lord. His faith was anchored in a war experience where he was shot at from twenty feet away and was not hit. He was convinced that the Lord would be with him in the present crisis. He "called upon the Lord" for healing but said that what he really wanted was that God's will be done.

All the evidence indicates that Dr. G's faith provided him with peace in the midst of turmoil. He was aware of no particular fear of death, and when the doctor told him that he was a rare person for being able to face his own death, he replied, "It is because I expect to be at home with the Lord when I die."[4] Dr. G had found the promise of life in death, and he died with the assurance that God would be with him all the way.

Both Mrs. K and Dr. G confront us with an interesting dilemma. It is difficult to say whether they have a simple faith or a refined faith. In actuality, they probably combine elements of both, but fortunately we do not have to decide before we can draw important lessons from their stories. Both Mrs. K and Dr. G indicate that the tenacity of faith can be indiscriminate. They seem to hold onto the pious beliefs of a simple faith as steadfastly as they hold onto the more sophisticated beliefs of a refined faith. In fact, a case could be made that as suffering increases or death draws near, they will be inclined to return to an early form of faith, no matter what it is. If that faith serves them well, they will hold onto it as they die. If, however, their faith fails to provide them with what they need, they may be motivated to re-examine their faith and, hopefully, to make it more encompassing.

Job is a biblical case in point. As Job struggles with God in the midst of unbearable suffering, he refuses to renounce his faith in spite of his wife's taunting to "curse God" (Job 2:9). He then spends most of his time struggling with God (when he is not defending himself against the untoward charges of his friends) and arrives at the point where he calls for a day in court where he can establish his innocence. He demands a chance to prove himself to God and to be relieved of his many sufferings. When God finally responds, Job gets more than he bargained for. God, speaking out of a whirlwind, confronts him with incomprehensible power and wisdom. Job gets the message and casts himself on God's mercy. "I am of small account. . . . I lay my hand on my mouth. . . . and repent in dust and ashes" (Job 40:4, 42:6). Job's faith has been transformed from a demand to a commitment. His growth in faith came as he walked along a precipice of unimaginable suffering. And Satan's prediction that Job believed only because he was richly blessed gave way to the greater truth that faith can be tenacious in its commitment, no matter what the circumstances.

THE BENEFITS OF A TENACIOUS FAITH

The tenacity of faith in someone who is facing death often surprises us. And yet we know that it is also true that death is too terrible to face without some kind of protective armor. Ernest Becker taught us this truth when he maintained that our sanity, or even our ability to live at all, presupposes that we have some kind of viable belief system.[5] So where death is concerned, we often find either denial or faith, either the pretense that death is not real or the assurance that it is not the final word. Faith is the better option. It provides hope in a hopeless situation and enables us to go through a dreadful situation with courage and confidence. It empowers us when all else fails and helps us to die without fear.

The advantage of faith centered in God is not simply that it provides us with an illusionary confidence. It is more positive, and certainly more awesome, than that. It puts death in a new light and gives us the resources to withstand its greatest assaults, not in any easy or automatic way but in a basic and enduring way. Faith in the God who raised Jesus from the dead takes the sting out of death in at least three ways: It breaks the power of death, overcomes the isolation of death, and diminishes the finality of death.

First, faith disarms the power of death. It aligns us with a God who is for life and who emerged victorious over death. This does not mean that death as physical cessation no longer haunts us, but it means that we do not die in despair, but instead we die in the promise of renewed life. In death, we find that God is with us, not against us.

Second, faith in a resurrection God dispels the isolation of death. We who believe do not die alone, but we die in Christ. Concretely, this means that we are gathered into a community and made a part of the household of God. In an earlier chapter, we observed that the prospect of death often separates us from others. As soon as people hear that we are terminally ill, they begin to pull away, leaving us all alone. Miss C's mother is a notable example.[6] She was diagnosed with a terminal illness and had to insist that she be allowed to die at home. Acceding to her wishes, the family prepared a first-floor bedroom for her down the hall from the kitchen. In the course of her illness, she told Miss C that she had two fears—dying alone and dying in the dark. One evening as Miss C was in the kitchen preparing dinner, she became aware of a dramatic change in her mother's condition. She knew that her mother needed her, but because she could not stand the thought of her mother dying, she did not walk down the hall. When she finally went to her mother, she found that she had died—alone and in the dark. Miss C lived with the guilt for years.

The mother's plight is an oft-repeated story, not because a loved one fails to walk down the hall but because both family and friends start pulling away at the prospect of death. They may be motivated by the need to protect themselves from grief as much as they are moved by the fear of death, but in any case the terminally-ill often die alone, if not in a physical sense than certainly in a personal and interpersonal sense.

Church members are not beyond abandoning the dying. Often we do not know what to say to someone who is sick unto death or we do not want to be reminded of our own mortality, so we avoid those who are seriously ill. Fortunately, there is another side to the church's reaction, a more helpful side. As a community of believers, we often stand by the dying person in a remarkable way. Through prayers, visitations, meals, and cards, we form a supportive web around the dying person and his or her family. We become a powerful and reassuring fellowship in which we acknowledge our mortality and share our hope in God's abiding presence.

At its best, the ministry of the Christian community approaches the example set by Mrs. M.[7] Mrs. M's husband did not want to die. Though he was losing a battle with cancer, he held out the hope that he could be with the family for some time to come. Nevertheless, his condition continued to worsen. One evening, after an especially difficult day, Mr. M asked if his children, ages four and six, could dance for him. Mrs. M got the children out of bed and had them perform one of Mr. M's favorite dances. Mr. M was pleased. His wife put the children back to bed and came down to sit with her husband. The scene that followed is described best in her own words:

> Mr. M wanted to hear me sing. I sang for him. He said he didn't want to die. I told him I loved him, and he said he loved me. Those were his last words. I reached out to hold his hand, and he got this pained look on his face and closed his eyes. He raised his hands over his chest, and then he just sighed and stopped breathing. All the time I was talking to him, telling him how much I loved him. I told him louder and louder when he closed his eyes, because I wasn't sure he could still hear me.

Mrs. M's faith enabled her to go a long way with her husband as he slid reluctantly toward death. She had the strength to fulfill his desire to experience familiar family events once more, like the boys dancing and her singing. She was able to stay with him, expressing love and lending support to the very end. Her actions were a concrete expression of her faith. "We always told the kids that if they ever got into trouble, or if they were ever scared, they should just close their eyes and know that we are right there with them. We are a part of them, just as God is always near to them and ready to help them."

Mrs. M's faith overcame the isolation of death by giving her the strength to be with her husband. Faith also overcomes death's isolation in another and broader sense. It puts us in touch with those who have gone before us. It maintains that we participate in, and are a part of, the communion of saints.

Often the church does not make as much of this fellowship as it should. About one day a year is set aside for remembering our deceased loved ones, most notably in early November on All Saints Sunday. The church also deals with death, more or less directly, when it conducts a funeral service, but generally death is not one of the church's favorite topics. In fact, the church may reflect society's tendency to avoid and deny death as much as possible.

Theologically, the church teaches that our departed brothers and sisters are not lost to us, that they belong to the church triumphant and that we are tied to them through our common faith in Christ. What the church often fails to advance is the great interconnection that we have with those who have died. We are part of a community of faith, specifically a part of a particular family that has a past and a future. We face death, then, not as an isolated entity but as a vital link in the ongoing activity of God. We are not a small cog in a giant machine but a personal concern to a God who lives and moves in human history. This declaration of faith may not make it easier to die, but it puts our death in proper perspective. We do not fall out of relationship with God and the community but instead become a living member of an ongoing fellowship.

The comfort of belonging to God as we face death has its antecedents in the Old Testament idea of covenant. The Israelites believed that God had made them his own by entering into a covenant with them. They viewed both life and death in terms of this covenant, which is to say that they believed that God gave them life and that God was more powerful than death. This faith did not rescue the

Israelites from having to struggle with death, but it gave them an anchor in the midst of the storm. They faced death with God rather than facing death alone. The promise that God makes to us in Baptism also means that we are God's own and that we die in the bosom of Christ.

The third and final way that the resurrection takes the sting out of death is that it diminishes the finality of death. It does not take death's finality away, but it assures us that death is already being addressed and subdued. Christ's resurrection is key here, and it is key because it gives us hope in an apparently hopeless situation by uniting us "with him in a resurrection like his" (Romans 6:5).

For Paul, Christ's resurrection or, more precisely, Christ being raised from the dead, is the peg on which everything else hangs. "If Christ has not been raised, your faith is futile and you are still in your sins. Then those also who have died in Christ have perished. If for this life only we have hoped in Christ, we are of all people most to be pitied" (1 Corinthians 15:17-19). Take the resurrected Christ away, and for Paul the Christian faith is destroyed. If Christ has not been victorious over death, then we are still under the condemnation of sin's death.

Paul's faith in the resurrection hope is reinforced by his expectation of Christ's return. He expected Christ to come back in his lifetime, for when he talks about "those who have died," he includes himself with those "who are alive, who are left" when Christ returns (1 Thessalonians 4:14, 17). Later, in addressing the Philippians, he talks of his desire to die and be with Christ, but he still seems to anticipate that he will be alive when Christ comes back. Christ's resurrection and his return are very real to Paul.

We live in a different world. We generally do not expect Christ to come any time soon. Further, because we live in a world that is dominated by scientific proof and see no admissible evidence of the resurrection, we become focused on the present. The church may still proclaim the risen Christ, but like the Apostle Thomas (John 20:25) we have our doubts. Without seeing Jesus raised, our faith in the resurrection as a viable and comforting antidote to the devastation of death is tested.

On the one hand, individually and collectively we systematically deny death, but on the other hand we spend a lot of energy trying to domesticate it. The space shuttle Challenger blows up and kills all seven people aboard, and we start an immediate investigation to find out what went wrong so it will not happen again. Two teenagers go on a rampage of violence, killing a number of innocent people, and we spend months trying to fathom the reasons why in order to prevent a reoccurrence. Every year, in reaction to the lethal effects of toys, cars, and a myriad other things, we enact laws that try to control the frequency, or even the occurrence, of death. Part of our reaction is appropriate and even responsible, but the insatiable drive to master death, and to try to eliminate it, is only an intense, this-worldly preoccupation with it.

Our preoccupation with death confronts us, and the church, with an important question, "Isn't death more real to us than sin? Aren't we more concerned with our mortality than we are with our separation from God?" In a way the question is false because sin and death cannot be split, at least not from a Pauline perspective where death is seen as the fruit of sin. Without denying the relationship between sin and death, we can still ask if death, not sin, is the point at which most of us feel vulnerable and threatened. I think the answer is "Yes." I believe that many people do struggle with sin and guilt, but more frequently than the church is willing to acknowledge, people are preoccupied with death.

It is the finality of death, the stark realization that an earthly life has ended, that often causes us the most sorrow.

As we stand at the graveside of a loved one, we know that this is the end of a life and a relationship. Actually, the whole funeral service, the closing of the casket, the words of the preacher, the remembrances of the deceased, the walk to the hearse, the lowering of the casket, is a series of events in which we say goodbye. This note of finality threatens meaninglessness, threatens to negate everything that we have affirmed about life. Small wonder that we stand in dire need of something that will diminish the finality of death.

Faith proposes an answer. A faith that is "foolish" and firm clings to the God who raised Jesus from the dead and rests in the hope that God will also raise us. It comes with no absolute guarantees, but it gives us a vantage point that transcends the possibility of being wiped out by death. It provides us with no provable promise, but it lends us courage and comfort in the face of our imminent demise. After all, we do not come to death with a lot of temporal resources that can withstand the devastation of death. In death's pain we wither, in its loss we doubt, and in its finality we grow weary and faint. But faith can be tenacious. It can stand firm against death. It reaches beyond our own resources and draws strength and assurance from the resurrected Christ, if not in a direct way then in and through the faith of the fellowship. "Now faith, hope, and love abide, these three" (1 Corinthians 13:13), but at the time of death the greatest need is to have faith.

THE PRACTICAL EXPRESSION
OF A TENACIOUS FAITH

Faith shows its tenacity by turning to prayer in times of trouble. It will not accept the situation as given, and it will not give up without recourse to God. Genuine prayer is a two-way conversation with God. We address God and

God addresses us. We must initiate the dialog, clarifying what we have in mind, but once we do we must listen for God's response. The tenacity that sends us to God in prayer should not close our ears to the Word that may stand over against us.

Mrs. Q, age twenty-one, came to the hospital with a case of uncontrolled diabetes. I was sent in to see her, because the nurse thought that she had been "pretty blue" for several days. A short distance into the visit, Mrs. Q spoke about "losing my baby." Furthermore, she said that members of a certain religious group had visited her and that they had said that since her baby was not baptized, it would not go to heaven. Mrs. Q did not know what to think, but the prospect of her child "just lying in the grave" sent her into depression.

About midway into the visit, Mrs. Q began to talk about the delivery. She said, "The doctors pronounced me dead on the operating table. No heart beat. No pulse." When asked what pulled her through, she responded, "I never lost my faith. I kept on praying and praying that I would get through this." I assumed that Mrs. Q was referring to a normal though difficult delivery. "Oh no," Mrs. Q corrected me, "the baby died three weeks before I went into labor. I was in the delivery room for three days and in labor for twelve hours." As Mrs. Q recalled the agony she fell silent. Her eyes moistened as she continued, "When they finally got the baby out, it had already started to disintegrate. But I kept on praying that they might be able to bring the baby back."

Mrs. Q witnesses to the tenacity of faith, both the good and the bad. She shows how faithfully a person can cling to God, asking for help, even on the threshold of death. Faith can give us a strength and a hope that ordinarily we would not have. But faith can also be tenacious in an unrealistic sense. It prompted Mrs. Q to pray for the fulfillment of a wish that had no basis in reality. In a similar vein, it can prompt us to pray for healing when healing is not possible, which is to say that it can prompt us to pray that our will be done and not God's. Job did not frame his request in the form of a prayer, but he, like all of us when we are suffering, looked for someone to vindicate him, someone to establish his innocence and to stop the apparent injustice. He called for an umpire, a witness to testify on his behalf when that was clearly not God's intended way to rescue him from suffering.

If the tenacity of faith finds practical expression in prayer, it is also true that the tenacity of faith is tested by prayer. What faith requests and hangs onto is either confirmed or denied. Mrs. Q illustrates both possibilities. Her request to survive the horrendous delivery was granted, but her unrealistic and impossible wish that the baby be returned to life was denied. Mrs. Q can decide, consciously or unconsciously, what she wants to hear. She can deny the unrealistic nature of her second petition and still hang onto the belief that her child could have been saved. If she does, she opts to affirm the tenacity of her faith against the overwhelming evidence of death or, more to the point, she decides not to grow in faith by gaining a greater understanding of God's working in the world and God's care for her.

The larger point is not what Mrs. Q will do but what we will do. Prayer often tests the tenacity—and the viability—of our faith. Many of our petitions to God are not answered, at least not in the way that we hope. Do we hang onto the expectations of our faith, or do we revise them to take into account God's way and will? Often God's will is not easy to discern (in fact, it may require prayerful consideration), but the basic issue at stake is the viability of our understanding of God. Are we in line with what God can possibly give us, or are we pursuing our perennial inclination to meet God and to relate to God on our own terms and with our own demands?

The tenacity of faith is manifested in both the heretic and the martyr. Both are willing to die for their faith, and both have done so in the church's history, so we know how tenacious the tenacity of faith can be. And yet it is not the tenacity of faith but the object of faith that defines faith's viability and value. For the Christian, the God who raised Jesus from the dead is the true center of our life and our hope. When faith clings to that God, it has a power all of its own.

CHAPTER 6

FAITH AND THE ASSURANCES OF GOD

MISS J,[1] AGE FORTY, SAT AT HER MAHOGANY desk and began to write to a friend. She always wrote to him when she was troubled, but this morning was especially bad. She had just returned from a visit with her mother, and her mother had done the usual "guilt trip" on her. As she leaned back in the chair, Miss J observed that life had always been "a series of hurdles to jump over with waning vitality." Whatever she did or whatever she achieved "was met sometimes with fleeting joy, but it was followed at once with doubting surprise, as 'mostly the work of chance.'" And in any case, "the inevitable flaw that it contained was held out and preyed upon, killing joy and nullifying the achievement by turning it into a mere appearance, a delusion, even a kind of lie."

Miss J was angry at herself. She had tried to reason with her mother, had tried to resist her mother's domination, but she should have known better. "The slightest questioning of her was a betrayal, and it was met with such demands for absolute trust and such outbursts of offended claims of integrity that it could shake, and make me doubt, the integrity of my own reason."

Miss J had hoped that her father would intervene and serve as a "counter influence," but it became apparent to her for the seventy times seventh time that he was "harassed by his own problems and had been reduced to a shadow of indifference because his self-image too had been shattered and destroyed."

The mother's trouble was obvious and long-standing. "Her claimant unhappiness, her terror of loneliness, her fear of being forsaken was a sort of obsessional intoxication of the very air" that Miss J breathed. And at the base of it all was the realization that she, Miss J, did not measure up to the mother's hopes and dreams. "If my sister was a desired child, my birth was welcomed as a little catastrophe. In some way, I failed my mother by insisting on coming into the world, and she did not get reconciled to the fact." Miss J lived with the realization that her mere existence was unacceptable to her mother. "Quite a few of the tearing contradictions and destructive events in my life can be traced back to an unconscious will to abort an unwanted life, if and when it could not be used to take vicarious revenge on me for her very real disappointment in me."

Miss J caught her breath. She looked up from the desk and through moist eyes saw an image of herself in the mirror. She had gotten up early to fix her hair and to dress up in one of her better outfits. But the image in the mirror spoke a different word. "I have failed. My best is never good enough. I feel guilty, and I am no good." Miss J's spirit was broken and her mother's oft-repeated words of abasement echoed in the wasteland. "You are just a swallow, and such a little bird carries no weight."

Miss J will have to wait a week before she hears back from her friend. She desperately needs his words of affirmation now, but she is too shattered to reach out for them—except to seal the envelope and drop it in the mail.

Miss J needs help, and if we were dealing with her directly we would try to be that help. But for now our interest is elsewhere. We are interested in Miss J's faith, specifically in what her faith offers her in terms of God's relation to her. In other words, we are going to use the case of Miss J to clarify and to expand our understanding of God as a resource in times of great suffering, whether or not Miss J actually experienced God in that way.

The Reformers, especially Martin Luther, tended to have a one-dimensional interest in God. They were interested in establishing God's unmerited grace over against any position that implied that we are saved by our own good deeds. Their concern is central to the gospel as Paul understood it, for indeed Paul never tired of emphasizing that our good standing before God is God's gift to us for Christ's sake, and not something we earn or deserve.

Unfortunately, the Reformers' position can easily be used to highlight God's work of redemption to the neglect of God's work of creation and of renewal. This emphasis is unfaithful to God's threefold relation to the world as Father, Son, and Holy Spirit, as the three articles in Luther's Small Catechism show.[2] It is also less than helpful on the level of our faith in God in times of crisis. Miss J will show us that in moments of great suffering we do not simply need the assurance that God forgives. We also need to know that God cares and that God renews or recreates. Anything less than this threefold assurance is not sufficient for our pastoral caring and is not exhaustive of the beneficent power of our faith.

THE ASSURANCE OF GOD'S CARE

Miss J did not die once. She died over and over as her mother tried to abort her life or tried to use it as a fulfillment of personal needs or as a target of endless hate. Miss J paid dearly for any attempt to be herself. Again and again what Miss J did was "twisted to fit with the image of failure and betrayal." Besides, Miss J adds, "My mother had a shattering, deadly accurate way of thrusting at, and enlarging, the one raw spot and thus of obliterating my very being."

Miss J must have wondered if anyone cared, if God cared. The cry became explicit when Miss J moved out of the house, and the mother enlisted the sympathy of friends and members of the church. She portrayed "to the last the image of her daughter betraying and forsaking her, 'crucifying' her motherly love and devotion." Even the pastor of the church reprimanded Miss J and played a part in having church members "pray for my repentance, for the confession and return of the prodigal daughter." Miss J, in a pathetic outburst, says, "No one cared about the way I would fare in all of this."

No one? Not even God?

In *Preaching God's Compassion: Comforting Those Who Suffer,*[3] Robert G. Hughes and I elaborate the way in which believers who are in the midst of suffering often feel that God is distant and unconcerned, that God is actually standing over against them to punish, to test, or to chasten them. Contrary to this stance, the Christian faith is bold enough—or foolish enough—to declare that God is with us in suffering. What we are talking about is an extension of the incarnation, the belief that God in Christ enters into our history and is with us in the actualities of our situation. It can be a great comfort to know that God is with us, even though, like Miss J, we may wonder if God really cares.

God's presence in suffering is part of a larger context of care. Martin Luther spells out that context in his Explanation to the First Article of the Apostles' Creed: "I believe that God has created me and all that exists; that He (sic) has given and still preserves to me . . . all my members, my reason and all the powers of my soul, . . . that He daily provides abundantly for all the needs of my life, protects me from all danger, and guards and keeps me from all evil."[4] In other words, God is not a distant Power who throws mere morsels to his subjects, but God is an ever-present Creator/Carer who nourishes and sustains us in every moment of life.

Paul makes God's caring presence even more personal. God is not only with us in suffering, but God actually suffers with us. Our suffering causes God to suffer. Or if Eberhard Jungel is right and death is the unfortunate end-point of our own drive toward relationlessness, God regrets our estrangement deeply and constantly reaches out to re-establish relationship with us and thus to mend the brokenness that ends in death. Suffering, then, or dying, is a sad and painful event for both God and us, which is to say that God is with us in suffering and in dying in a profound and personal way. In an earlier discussion, we elaborated this assurance by introducing Martin Luther's concept of the theology of the cross (see page 50).

For Luther, the theology of the cross is not one theological theme among other theological themes, not even if it has to do with the central doctrine of the atonement. Instead the death and resurrection of Jesus becomes a lens through which the whole content of the faith is seen. At the heart of "God with us" is the declaration that "Christ is risen" or, more precisely, that Christ was raised from the dead by God, in order to rescue us from the extinction of death. God is Lord of both life and death. The faith that hangs onto this belief is assured that nothing, not even death, can destroy us or can gain final victory over us, because there is no falling out of God's care, no being out of relationship with God, even in death. Like a lamb in the arms of a shepherd, we are safe and secure in God's presence. "Where, O death, is your victory? Where, O death, is your sting?" (1 Corinthians 15:55)

If faith knows the assurance of God's providential care, it also knows the dark night of the soul when faithful believers experience the despair that Miss J experienced. Job becomes the brunt of Satan's torments and laments, "Let the day perish in which I was born, and the night that said, 'A man-child is conceived'. . . . Why did I not die at birth, come forth from the womb and expire?" (Job 3:3, 11). Ecclesiastes surveys the futility of human toil and knowledge and cries out, "Then I considered all that my hands had done and the toil I had spent in doing it, and again, all was vanity and a chasing after wind, and there was nothing to be gained under the sun" (Ecclesiastes 2:11). Luther experienced what he called *anfechtung,* moments of doubt and panic when he felt abandoned by God. He found those moments almost unbearable, because they represented a crisis within faith itself. They amounted to an internal struggle "between doubt in a God who seems to have abandoned us and faith in a loving God who overcomes pain and death" in and through Christ.[5] Luther never found a final solution to these moments, but he knew "that any reliance on his own resources did not help but in fact often aggravated the despair."[6] What sustained him in those moments, and what made them occasions of growth in faith, was to rely totally on the external promise of God's Word. Against the voice that accused him, he cast himself on the fact that Christ died for him. In other words, by the thin thread of faith he faced into the despair and hung onto a caring and crucified God.

THE ASSURANCE OF GOD'S GRACE

Miss J was acquainted with guilt, even to the point of feeling guilty for existing at all. She also felt the condemnation of guilt, the sense of "I am no good" with its attendant feelings of unworthiness and deceit. She got "caught in a whirlpool of contention between God the Torturer and God the Giver of Life." In a poignant moment of despair, she confesses, "More heart-broken than afraid, I see within that inner space of the heart, the despairing Shadow trying to exist without God, i.e., against God, shut up within her limitations, blind to the Life without which her very existence would not 'be.' This is what it means to be by nature sinful and unclean. *There* is sin, and it literally implies Death—the Shadow, like a little ball of derived energy, exists, whirling upon itself, with its void center."

Miss J's confession—and it is a confession at the same time that it is a cry of despair—is remarkable in its own right. In many respects, Miss J can be seen as a passive victim of her mother's rejection and destruction. Seen in this way, we might conclude that Miss J is not guilty, that she is more sinned against than sinner. In one important respect, however, she is like us. She tries to exist without God, tries to make it on her own. She recognizes that the attempt is an act of sin, and that the result—life without God—is death, is a pseudoexistence that whirls around a void center. The whole situation is both unfair and tragic. Miss J is unjustly victimized and tries to survive by her own power, but in taking matters into her own hands she has separated herself from God even as she stands in dire need of God's help.

The only answer to this dilemma is the assurance of God's grace, the conviction that God understands Miss J's plight and that God accepts her in spite of her part in the tragedy. God's grace is not a cure-all for the situation. It may not even change the outward situation very much, but it gives Miss J a claim on acceptance and acceptability that can soften, or even disarm, the mother's harshest words.

To achieve this effect, the assurance of God's grace may have to be mediated through a human relationship. In Miss J's case, the mediation came through a friend, through a person of some stature in the church who faithfully stood by her and who genuinely prized her as one of God's own. In other cases, the mediation may come through a pastor, a chaplain, or a pastoral counselor who in words or deeds may communicate God's love or may incarnate it in concrete form. Laypersons may be especially effective, for they may have daily contact with Miss J and in their unofficial ministry to her may witness to God's spontaneous and unconditional identification with her suffering—what Martin Luther calls the "mutual conversation" and consultation of the brothers and sisters.[7]

We have returned to a point that Paul made in chapter 1. Faith not only clings to God's grace. It also gives expression to God's grace. It is a concrete expression of love and service to the neighbor in need in an attempt to address the neighbor's greatest need and to build up not only the neighbor but also the fellowship as a whole. Faith active in love encourages faith in the recipient and empowers him or her to cling to God's promise of forgiveness and affirmation. Miss J's friend stood over against the destructive words of the mother and became a medium through which Miss J experienced the assurance of God's grace. We can experience that assurance in the Sunday service in the pronouncement of absolution, in the proclamation of the Word, and in the prayers for those who are alone or defeated.

The Assurance of God's Renewal

Miss J's whole struggle came to a head when her mother died unexpectedly. She writes to her friend: "My mother died quietly and suddenly the day after my return from a vacation. I got home and found no news. I phoned. My mother was 'not too bad,' only some new medicine was causing a 'little digestive trouble.'" Miss J decided to take the morning train instead of the night train. "When I arrived, she was gone—in a slumber without suffering. I kissed her cold forehead and gazed at her strangely young-looking face."

Initially, Miss J experienced "a strange quietness, a dull sadness but no brokenness." She continues: "What should have been broken [at her death] was broken many years ago, and I have mourned for her spirit ever since. The mysterious warfare that her spirit waged against mine was relentless to the end. My quest for the meaning and the truth of it will continue, perhaps as relentlessly."

Miss J's friend received no letters from her for a month. When she finally broke the silence, she said. "I am sorry I could not write to you sooner, but I have been 'winged' for the past three weeks, caught unaware by a minor breakdown. I feel better now, a part of the human race again."

The mother's death aroused a question that Miss J had probably asked herself many times. "Can God change a tragic situation into something new? Can God bring life out of death?" She admits, "Now that mother has gone, I do not know what God wants to do with me. I cannot truthfully say that I have faith that God wants 'to love me forward into myself.' This self has been severed at the very roots of my being, its life regretted for so long that it has become arrested and disfigured."

Even as Miss J records her doubt, she points to the way. "What I needed was a 'counter-influence.' Instead there was no illumination, no light-bearer along the way." She has forgotten. When she reflects back on her breakdown, she writes to her friend, "I hung onto your words as a hook of life over a precipice."

We could go on to detail Miss J's gradual recovery to the point where she became an effective elementary teacher, but we want to speak more generally about God's third blessing to us, about God's renewing power in the midst of suffering.

Ever since seminary days, I have been enamored by the Greek word *dynamis*. In the mouth of my New Testament professor, the sound of the word almost portrayed what the word was all about, namely, "power," the kind of power that gave us the English word dynamite.

The Holy Spirit is the *dynamis* ("power") of the Godhead. It is not the cruel power to smite or the aggressive power to dominate but the sanctifying power to empower, that is, the power to give life or to give understanding or to give courage.

In Scripture whenever the Spirit moves, things happen. The Spirit of God sweeps over the formless face of the earth, and it becomes a vibrant planet filled with form and life (Genesis 1:1-31). The angel Gabriel announces to Mary, "The Holy Spirit will come upon you, and the power of the Most High will overshadow you," and she becomes the mother of Jesus (Luke 1:35). At Jesus' baptism, "the heaven was opened, and the Holy Spirit descended upon him," and he became God's "Son, the Beloved" (Luke 3:21-22). After spending forty days in the wilderness, "Jesus, filled with the power of the Spirit, returned to Galilee" and began his ministry by teaching in the synagogues (Luke 4:14-15). After his resurrection, when Jesus was ready to send his disciples into the world, "he breathed on them and said to them, 'Receive the Holy Spirit,'" and they received the power to forgive sins in Jesus' name (John 20:22-23).

The Holy Spirit is the *dynamis* of God and makes things happen.[8]

Our primary concern is not with the general work of the Holy Spirit as he calls, gathers, and enlightens the Christian church. Our concern is with the work of the Holy Spirit as faith encounters and comes to terms with death. Concretely, we need to reflect on the church's ministry to those who struggle with diminished life.

To all appearances, death seems like an end, especially if our faith has turned frail. When we are in the throes of death, we are not interested in or comforted by paradoxical statements like "gain can come out of loss, and life can emerge out of death." Death seems too final. We are drained of all strength and courage, and, like Ivan Ilych, we can only stand before death and shudder.

And yet there is another side, a truly unexpected and paradoxical side to death. A nineteen-year-old student, home from college for the summer, speeds over a hill late at night and slams into an on-coming car. He dies instantly. His father is on a business trip; his mother is home and receives the call. She thinks of her pastor and awakens him at three AM. The pastor rushes to the mother's side as fast as he can. The mother, struggling not to collapse, expresses her grief in torrents of disbelief and agony. She is devastated and defeated, and yet through it all she is strengthened and comforted.

We know that the actual situation is far more complex than this brief vignette implies, but it says what many believers experience—that in the midst of turmoil, even in the face of unimaginable horror, believers find strength and hope in and through their faith. Dietrich Bonhoeffer, who was imprisoned in Nazi Germany for two years and who was under the constant threat of death, lived and served his fellow inmates in relative tranquility. The day before he was put to death, he conducted a worship service for the prisoners. As he was led away by "two evil-looking men," he drew a friend aside and said, "This is the end. For me the beginning of life."[9] His faith, his tranquility is incomprehensible to the human mind. His courage defies all rational thought and seems like the ultimate expression of denial and self-deception.

Shock and denial are an inextricable part of an individual's reaction, especially if death comes suddenly like it did to the mother of the teenager. Alongside this truth, however, is the observation that faith has strengthened saints and sinners alike down through the ages. We see the empowerment repeated today in the meek and merciful who believe in their hearts and confess with their lips that their faith has pulled them through. We are talking about the work of the Holy Spirit, about the power of God to arouse and sustain faith in blatant contradiction to the powers that would defeat us.

The theological textbooks say that the Holy Spirit works through the proclamation of the gospel and the administration of the sacraments. In a foundational sense that is true. Both Word and Sacraments declare "forgiveness of sins, resurrection of the flesh, and eternal life,"[10] and the Holy Spirit works through these means to stir up faith in the believer. What these theological statements need is flesh and bone. The statements do not acknowledge as much as they should that the Holy Spirit works through people, drawing them into a fellowship, a communion of saints where Word and Sacrament bear the promise of grace in the lives of people.

When I was eight years old, my aunt Kate died at the age of forty-three while giving birth to her sixth child. The funeral was held at home—in a small farmhouse filled with friends and relatives. My uncle sat by the casket and sobbed, filling the room with the torture of untimely death. I do not remember many of the events of the day, but I can still hear my uncle giving expression to his grief.

I did not comprehend much about death at the time, but from my uncle's reaction I got the feeling that death was horribly tragic and that there was a great need to bring help or comfort to the situation. My eight-year-old mind did not go so far as to reflect on the strength of my uncle's faith, but the whole experience left me with certain definite impressions. I saw that death topples everything in its path, including my uncle; that the people gathered there, including my parents, needed to be there; and that the minister was trying to bring order and hope to a chaotic scene.

Reflecting on the experience now, I see other dynamics. I see that the minister was proclaiming the hope of the resurrection even though the people at that moment were more wrapped up in their own grief and loss than they were in the possibility of life after death. I see that the people needed to be there, not just because they were bonded together in a common loss but also because they were comforting each other even while they were being comforted by each other. I see that the people who were gathered there were as mortal and fragile as the aunt who was lying in the casket and that therefore any strength and hope that was experienced had to come from Someone who had gone through death and had defeated it. I see that when the funeral service was over the people had to regroup to eat and to talk together, not as a way to deny death but as a way to affirm life in the midst of death. I see that the Holy Spirit was at work in, with, and under the trials and the tears of a grieving fellowship.

There are moments in the work of the Holy Spirit when terminally-ill patients are strengthened or when mourners are comforted, but generally the work of the Holy Spirit is ongoing and ever-present, even as a life-long struggle. When we say that God is Lord of both life and death, we may experience a certain relief from the threat of death, but to put one's life and one's death unconditionally in God's hands and live free from the terror or sadness of death is quite a different thing. The resurrection as a concept may sound good, but to live and to die in the firm hope of the resurrection is achieved at the end of a struggle, not at its beginning. The work of the Holy Spirit does not conform to our linear vision. Growth in faith is not a developmental but a paradoxical phenomenon.

Under ordinary circumstances, we tend to think that growth in faith is progressive, that we move from being troubled by a God who limits or judges us to accepting and loving a God who preserves and supports us. We may grant that there is a back-and-forth movement along the continuum, but we anticipate that the general direction during the course of our life will be toward greater faith in God. In this scheme of things, we can locate ourselves somewhere along the continuum at any one time with a fair degree of precision, and we never move far enough to the left or the right to negate the opposite possibility. If, for example, we are filled with doubt, even to the point of thinking that God has abandoned us, we still manifest faith, maybe not in a good and loving God but in a God who has turned temporarily away from us. In any case, we never live without some degree of faith, and according to the ground plan we should become increasingly more mature in our faith.

Luther had a different experience in his struggles with *anfechtung*.[11] Miss J, too, found no steady progress toward increased faith in God. "My faith in the love of God remained unimpaired for a long time, but then I began to ask, 'Where is he?' What really became crippling was the silence of God in the midst of anguish, the absence of some counter influence as if some delicate 'instrument of communication' had been broken beyond repair, and I was now unfit for life." Miss J lived between faith and doubt, and often doubt gained the upper hand.

My father also wavered between faith and doubt. He got emphysema when he was fifty-three and struggled with it until he died twenty-five years later. The disease got progressively worse, so that my father went from being a strong and independent person to being an emaciated and dependent patient. Because faith is, or can be, a private affair, I do not know the nature of my father's faith at the beginning of his illness. I know that he attended church regularly, that he served willingly on several committees of the church, and that he did not seem too restless when my mother insisted on daily devotions. As the emphysema progressed, however, my father became more impatient and resentful. Like Luther, his struggle with faith seemed to be a paradoxical situation in which faith and doubt interacted with each other. This paradoxical situation continued for many years until the last year or two of his life when his faith was no match for his moments of doubt and despair. He was overwhelmed by the seeming injustice and the endless torture of his illness. He could not reconcile the goodness and love of God with what was happening to him.

My father's failure of faith may not be unusual in such dire circumstances, but neither does it negate the many times in which suffering leads to increased faith. What it shows is the precariousness and unpredictability of the journey. The work of the Holy Spirit, though powerful and persistent in its own right, seems to be rendered powerless by our human situation. That, however, is not the end of the story.

Our faith, or lack of it, is not God's final word. Even if our faith no longer appears to grasp onto God's grace and power, God is active in our situation. Luther found great comfort in God's actions, and he located the action concretely in our Baptism, not because Baptism was a magical act that made everything all right but because it was a sacramental expression of God's care and love for us. Through Baptism, we are adopted as children of God and as God's children we are heirs to the gifts of the Spirit—forgiveness of sins, resurrection of the body, and life everlasting.

I am sure that being Baptized was not a comfort to my father. He was not mindful of God's initiative in Baptism, and he never arrived at the point where, like Luther, he could simply cling to God's promises no matter what the circumstances. But the fact that my father was Baptized was a comfort to me. As I saw his faith grow weary in the scorched valley of suffering, I found assurance in the shade of God's promise to be with him in life and in death. I could see what my father in his suffering could not see—moments of grace and great care, moments when the Holy Spirit was empowering doctors, loved ones, and friends to bring relief and love to a hopeless situation. In my mother's faithful care of my father, in my sister's empathic understanding of him, in our neighbors' concern for him, and in our relatives' support of all of us, I saw the power of God manifested in the midst of my father's desperate situation. In all of this, I never thought it was my duty, or the pastor's duty for that matter, to remind my father of God's caring presence. Instead it was my duty to be God's caring presence to my father, to sit with him in his helplessness and to be present to him as an incarnated concretion of God's promise of power and renewal.

As we have seen, God has a threefold relation to the world, and thus God represents a threefold assurance for those who struggle with the lessening, even the termination, of life. God sustains with suffering care, God redeems with unearned mercy, and God comforts and renews with sanctifying power. If, then, as we approach the brink of death, we ask, "Where is God?" faith assures us that God is suffering with us and is caring for us. If we ask, "What did I do to deserve this?" faith assures us that Christ has already paid the price of our sins. And if we ask, "How will we get through this?" faith assures us that God is working to empower us and to renew us. This is the mighty power of God, and this is the power of faith as it clings to God. We are called to incarnate this power in our relationship with the needy neighbor; otherwise, that power may never become real to the person who desperately needs it.

CHAPTER 7

THE PSYCHOLOGICAL FRUITS OF FAITH

IN CHAPTER 1, I INTRODUCED PAUL'S CONCEPT of faith as obedience. Paul maintains that faith is not an act unto itself, that it does not simply grasp onto God's grace and remain dormant. On the contrary, it is impelled into the world where it serves the neighbor in need in order to build up the fellowship of believers.

Luther picked up Paul's concept and maintained that faith leads "with inner necessity, to 'works,'. . . to joyfully serving God by serving the neighbor."[1] According to Luther one way to determine if faith is really genuine is to see whether or not it flows into works of love. Luther is not being inconsistent with his contention that the sinner is justified by faith alone. He is talking about what happens after justification. The individual is so thankful to be forgiven by God and so empowered by the Spirit that he or she goes into the world to serve the neighbor whenever the neighbor is in need. Faith after justification, then, has a two-sided relation to works. On the one hand, it becomes the source out of which serving the neighbor flows, and on the other hand, it is authenticated as genuine by its service to the neighbor. Luther is acknowledging that faith can be false, can be imagined and self-fabricated, but he is also saying that if it is genuine it reflects and manifests the spirit of Christ himself, the spirit of serving as Christ himself served.

Paul and Luther point to the primary fruit of faith, at least in terms of faith's gift to the fellowship of believers. Faith loves and serves the community. Without minimizing this gift, we want to focus on what faith does for the believer who faces death. What are the fruits of faith when it encounters death, either one's own death or the death of a loved one? We think that in grasping onto God's grace, faith not only effects the self's relation to God and the neighbor but it also effects the self's relation to itself. Specifically, it empowers the self in a threefold psychological sense: It enables the self to accept what was, to live with what is, and to embrace what is to come.

ACCEPTING WHAT WAS

Erik Erikson, a developmental psychologist, highlights the importance of being able to accept our life as we have lived it. He maintains that as our potency, performance, and adaptability decline in old age, we are confronted with the need to become what he calls a person of mature integrity. For him, this means at least two things. On the one hand, it means that we are able to face the ambiguity of life, to acknowledge and assimilate both the "triumphs and disappointments of being, by necessity, the originator of others and the generator of things and ideas."[2] In short, we can see and experience ourselves as a mixture of success and failure. On the other hand, integrity means that we possess a genuine sense of satisfaction with our life, that we are content with and are able to accept both the determinations that have shaped us and the self-determinations by which we have shaped ourselves. Both meanings, taken together, describe a person who has a genuine and deep-seated acceptance of life as that life has been lived and experienced.

According to Erikson, failure to achieve this sense of satisfaction means that we may struggle with feelings of bitterness and incompleteness. We resent the many limitations of life and cannot acknowledge death as our imminent and final fate. For Erikson, the outcome of the struggle is determined in good part by our developmental history, by the degree to which we have successfully maneuvered earlier developmental tasks (stages). But we are not locked into a predetermined end. We can take steps to rework our history, not by erasing unacceptable details but by changing our response to them.

Faith in God's care and mercy provides us with a new perspective on our past. In chapter 1, I said that death prompts us to examine what we have done with the life that we have been given. Not everyone who faces death may go through a life review, but many of us do, sometimes on a private level where our loved ones are not aware of it. In fact, we can go through the process without ourselves being fully aware of it. In any case, to review our life, what we have done and not done, in the light of God's good news is to be able to accept it for what it is. We can celebrate our accomplishments and can acknowledge our defeats without either one of them being a measure of our personal adequacy or an indication of our standing before God.

Faith not only gives us a new perspective on our past. It also influences the way in which we review the past. Remembering the past is not a single and monolithic activity. In actuality, there are at least three kinds of remembering, and it is the third kind of life review that seems especially helpful in preparing for death.

First, there is the kind of remembering that older people often do. It is talking about the past, usually in an objectified or even in a repetitious, way. It makes the past something out there, something that happened a long time ago. Remembering in this sense is mostly telling a story about what happened, or supposedly happened, without really being interpersonally involved. The self remembers, either to escape the present or to glorify the "good old days." In short, this kind of remembering tends to be characterized by detachment and is used to serve the interests of the storyteller. As such, it is a reassurance against the desolation of old age but not a preparation for death.

Second, there is a remembering at the other end of the spectrum. It is the remembering of psychoanalysis or of most therapeutic endeavors. It is designed to help us get in touch with the past, to recall it and to own it. It deals with experiences that have been repressed or denied, because they were unacceptable to the self. This kind of remembering is often a long and difficult process of overcoming defenses and resistances, so that the person's past can be comprehended and owned in its complexity and detail. It can help to clear the obstacles that are in the way to a fuller life, but it seldom serves as preparation for death, and it certainly does not domesticate the sting of death.

The third kind of remembering is not a repetitious or objective recall of the past. It is also not an intricate recall of repressed material. Instead, it is an existential, often a spontaneous, reliving of past relationships. It is holding someone who is dear in remembrance and re-experiencing shared meanings and notable events. It is getting in touch with one's world and being touched by it.

Remembering in this sense has more to do with "our life together" than it does with how we feel about this or that. Specific feelings about significant events or persons are important, but generally they belong to the second kind of remembering. Remembering in the third sense deals with a world that was. It focuses on significant events or persons and acknowledges the particular meaning that they had for us. Nicholas Wolterstorff's *Lament for a Son*[3] is an illustration of this kind of remembering. Of course, Wolterstorff deals with particular feelings about his son's death, but mostly he holds his son in remembrance and relives the life he had with him and now the life that is gone. His remembrances are poignant and serve at least three purposes: They review and relive the past; they are a tribute to the deceased and an acknowledgment of his importance to the family; and they recognize the absence of the deceased and are a foretaste of life without him.

The importance of the third kind of remembering is described in similar fashion by a former student, who recalls the death of a friend and reflects on the time she spent with her friend's family as they looked through photo albums, videos, letters, and memorabilia. "We spent several days together exchanging pictures and stories, and discussing aspects of the funeral and reception. I cried buckets of tears, but I also laughed because I could not escape the beauty of our friendship, and the fun and momentous times we had shared."

The student describes some of the major conditions that make remembering an effective instrument of healing: It is centered on the deceased in his or her concrete aliveness; it is a fellowship of shared meanings where mourners walk through the valley of suffering with each other; and it is a re-working of lost relationships, because it deals with stories about the deceased and is focused on what was and implicitly on what is no more.

The student's description of the value of remembering is focused on the process of grief, but much of what she says can be transferred to our struggle with death and dying. Remembering in the shadow of death brings our life into the light. It recalls significant events and meaningful relationships, acknowledging our disappointments and celebrating our joys. It is not an extended analysis of the past but a series of intermittent snapshots in our mind. In this sense, they are a neat summary of who we are and of what we have been. They also point to our place in the family or the community and illuminate the meaning that we had for them and for ourselves. Implicitly if not explicitly, they acknowledge our impending death and help us to live out a fitting end to our existence.

At its best, the third kind of remembering relates our life to God. It represents an opening of our life to God, a placing of our past in the hands of God. This is important, because both our impending death and our review of life raise ultimate questions. Why am I dying? Why did I live? What is the meaning of it all? What will happen to me after I die? Most of us are unable to give a satisfying answer to these questions. We therefore look beyond ourselves for a framework, a relation of trust in which we can begin to get some answers to these questions. And when the answers reach the end of their explanatory power, we simply put our life in God's hands. We live by faith, believing that the triune God has sustained us in our living, has forgiven us in our failure, and has renewed us in our losses. This faith has the power to comfort us. We are assured of God's enduring love, and we can affirm our past with its disappointments and its victories as a gift that we have received and experienced.

LIVING WITH WHAT IS
Faith not only helps us to affirm the past, but it also helps us to live in the present. "One day at a time" is the watchword

of AA. It enables those who are addicted to alcohol to concentrate their efforts on the immediate situation instead of focusing on the formidable task of staying sober day after day. Living a day at a time has also become the password of the Hospice movement. Hospice, an international program for the care of the dying and their families, seeks to help terminally-ill patients increase the quality of life rather than being preoccupied with its length. It empowers patients and families to live in the present by creating an atmosphere in which they and their families can work together to make the most of life while it lasts. The program includes an honest acknowledgment of the approach of death and a discussion of its meaning for the patient and the family. The goal is to help the patient die with dignity and a sense of self-worth within a circle of familial support.

Psychotherapy, too, tries to empower the person to live in the present instead of being stuck in the past or escaping into the future. It is not against acknowledging the past or planning for the future, but it has found that we often clutter up the present with unresolved issues or undue expectations. Instead of being able to give ourselves to the moment and enjoying its possibilities and richness, we get away from life as it is and dwell in some wished-for world.

Actually, psychotherapy shows that there are at least two primary ways in which we clutter up the present. One is when unresolved issues from the past live in and distort the present, and the other is when we load the present with undue and unrealistic expectations. Sigmund Freud unearthed the first impediment; Karen Horney the second one. We need to give brief attention to both.

Freud and the Distortion of the Present
Freud maintained that we humans tend to repress unacceptable desires or impulses; that is, we tend to keep them out

of consciousness and to prevent them from seeking satisfaction. The initial force that prompts repression may be positive and constructive, for repression is often undertaken as a means of avoiding or resolving a potentially embarrassing, or even a threatening, situation. In this sense, it is a life-saving attempt to avoid desires that are unacceptable to us.

No matter how positive the intention of repression, its immediate and long-term result is harmful and enslaving. It creates a division within us, a cleavage between repressed desires and rational and moral judgment. We become dominated by an inner estrangement, living on the socially-acceptable surface of ourselves while denying our deeper needs and desires.

According to Freud, the repression of desires does not strip them of their driving power. They continue to exist and manifest themselves in our thoughts, words, or deeds. They come out in devious and indirect ways, expressing themselves in our daily life as slips of the tongue, neurotic symptoms, crippling phobias, unsettling dreams, and a myriad other forms. The upshot of this development is that the individual is tied to his or her past; that is, he or she lives in, and responds to, the present in terms of some previously unassimilated desire or experience.

This bondage to the past and this distortion of the present can be illustrated by many examples. The hungry child's wish for ice cream is not granted, but in his sleep he dreams of falling into a large bowl of it. A spouse does not take time to mourn the loss of a partner, but when the family suffers the loss of a pet she goes into a deep and prolonged depression. A family member loses a job under circumstances that reflect on his or her competence, but instead of expressing the feelings directly, he or she flies off the handle when a friend makes a casual comment about the inadequacy of an acquaintance. The untimely reaction to present events often takes more complex forms, but the point is illustrated. Thoughts or experiences that are repressed at the time they happen can continue to exist and can distort our perception of, and our reaction to, present circumstances or events.

Freud's insight is directly applicable to our struggle with death. In an earlier chapter, we said that in some sense death casts a shadow on our life, but we also observed that life can cast a shadow on our dying. Events or relationships in life that remain troubling or unassimilated may haunt our dying days and distort the way in which we view, and react to, the prospect of death. If we have had a series of losses and have not come to terms with them, that history may aggravate the loss posed by our own impending death. As we struggle with death, we may struggle not only with our own demise but also with the earlier loss of loved ones whom we never mourned. In other words, we may be mourning previous deaths as much as we are mourning our own. Our grief is not only misplaced but also is unduly heavy and unfruitful.

We could maintain that often death is such an unpleasant and unwanted experience that it is good not to live in the present if it means living our dying. There may be truth to this argument, since sliding out of existence is not necessarily a cherished prospect or process. But living in the present is not primarily about dying. It is about living life today. It is about meeting the current situation with all the internal and external resources that we have at our disposal. It means living life as long as it lasts and giving ourselves to the treasurers of the moment, to the memories shared, to the relationships enjoyed, to the love and comfort received. In this sense, living in the present is living life to the fullest, even as we approach the point at which it will be taken away.

Horney and the Tyranny of the Should[4]

Karen Horney adds another perspective to our distortion of the present. She maintains that if we live in an environment that makes it difficult for us to pursue our needs and possibilities, we tend to initiate a substitute process of growth to provide us with a sense of unity and relatedness. The substitute process, called neurosis, represents a change of direction in the core of the self. Instead of trying to actualize our real potentialities, we strive to realize an unlimited and glorified version of ourselves by idealizing everything we are and do. Our hopes, our achievements, our behaviors, and our relation to others are cast in the image of the ideal. Horney calls it a comprehensive search for glory in which we reach for the absolute. We assume that our willpower should be unshakable, our reasoning infallible, our foresight flawless, and our knowledge all encompassing.

Reality stands over against our wishes. Try as we may, we cannot fashion ourselves as we want, for both the limitations of our own being and the actualities of the impinging world remind us that our life has not been remade to conform to our wish for infinite realization. According to Horney, we have two ways to muffle the message of reality. The first one, effective against the actualities of the world, is called "neurotic claims"; the second one, effective against the limitations of self, is called "the tyranny of the should." It is the second way that is especially relevant to our concern.

"The tyranny of the should" refers to insatiable inner dictates that operate on the premise "that nothing should be, or is, impossible for"[5] us. Such dictates are completely insensitive to the actual conditions under which we can find genuine fulfillment. Instead our whole life revolves around what ought to be, for we are dominated by the relentless demand that we should be different and more perfect than we really are. We are driven by what we "should be able to do, to be, to feel, to know."[6] In this sense, the "shoulds" are different than genuine ideals, for they are permeated by a spirit of egoism and are dominated by a spirit of coercion. Instead of urging us toward the actualization of our real selves, they destroy spontaneous growth, disturb relationships with others, and force us to live a life of insatiable demands.

Concrete examples are abundant. Instead of enjoying the success of the moment, John minimizes his achievement and actually berates himself for not achieving more. Joan sticks with a demanding diet and loses a pound a week for several months, but all the while she demands more of herself and refuses to say that the diet is working. A mother devotes hours of care to her ailing child, even to the point of sacrificing her own needs, but she does not think that she is doing enough and sees the child's failure to improve as her own failure.

These are only a few instances of Horney's point. They highlight the way we bankrupt the present by measuring it against the standards of what ought to be. We live in the hope that we will do better the next time and that eventually we will succeed in being and doing the ideal. This means, in effect, that we get bogged down in guilt that is enflamed by our unrealistic and inordinate expectations and rendered unforgivable by our unrelenting and insatiable demands. In effect, we never fully live in the present. Our energies are preempted, our aspirations are skewed, our very selves are distorted or abandoned.

This whole scenario distorts the dying process. We cannot die with any sense of worth. We cannot live in the present, because it is paled by the intense inner dictates of what we think we ought to be or do. We cannot affirm life, because in fact we are engaged in a process that means the death of who we really are. We die in the stranglehold of guilt and regret, unable to accept the forgiveness of God because we are bound by an overwhelming sense of failure and personal unworthiness. This is one of the radical ways in which our life can distort our dying. It can shut us off from the very gift that Christ came to give us, namely, freedom from our own feverish attempts to make ourselves acceptable.

EMBRACING WHAT IS TO COME

Finally, faith does something to our relationship with the future. It empowers us to trust whatever lies beyond the horizon. It may seem strange to say that we should trust the future when we are on the threshold of death. If we only had our earthly days in mind, it would be strange, but we also have in mind God's plan for us beyond our present existence. This is where our final trust should be—in the God who has prepared rooms for us.

To trust God is not something that we may find easy to do as death approaches. In fact, it may come, if at all, only at the end of a hard battle, only when all else fails. But when it comes, what does it look like? What does it mean to trust God's future? Ironically, whatever else it means, it is to trust death itself as the gateway to new life.

We may live with a concrete picture of what it means to trust death. We may know someone, perhaps an older person or maybe even a younger person, who went quietly and confidently into the night. They were ready to meet the Lord, as they put it, and as we stood by them we admired their courage at the same time that we questioned their sincerity. "How could anyone die with such assurance?" Maybe we suspect that there is a good deal of denial going on, but beyond that what was happening? Whatever it was, it was not necessarily apparent to the unaided eye. After all, it is a miracle of a sort that a living creature can slide peacefully and confidently into non-existence. It is this "miracle" that interests us. We may not plumb its depths, but we want to reflect on some of its more important aspects.

We can start by considering the idea that death itself may help us die. Or to put it in religious terms: God has built into the dying process a preparation for death. Maybe something like this belief is common knowledge among medical people, but I think most of us underestimate, or even deny, the extent to which death signals its approach and prepares us for it. People know that they are going to die. They may misjudge the exact time of death, but just as a sick person has a fairly accurate sense of how serious his or her condition is, so a person who is dying may know that the end is near. There is nothing very mysterious about this. The dying process is a particular kind of process with its own physiological and psychological dynamics. All we have to do is tune into that process, admit it into consciousness, and allow it to happen. In this sense, then, death is not a foreign invasion. It is an internal happening, something that God may have put into the design to help us through the ordeal.[7]

Dying involves a letting-go. Kubler-Ross describes something like this in her fifth and final stage of dying— the stage of acceptance. She describes acceptance as a time of withdrawal from friends and family, a time when the patient longs for, and enters into, a "final rest before the long journey."[8] What is missing in Kubler-Ross's description is what may be going on inside the patient. Maybe the patient's withdrawal is not just a "void of feelings," as she suggests, but a more positive state of letting-go and resting in the arms of something or somebody, maybe even in the arms of the dying process itself. For the Christian, it is resting in the mercy and promises of God. The dying process itself may help us to get there. By stripping away our energies and our defenses and making us passive recipients, it prepares us to admit that our lives are in the hands of God.

Again, Tolstoy's Ivan Ilych[9] illuminates the point. Ivan Ilych is terminally-ill and goes through a prolonged struggle with different dimensions of that reality. Finally, he arrives at the threshold of death. As he stands there, he is concerned about the goodness of his life, the way in which his life must have amounted to something. He is determined to defend his accomplishments, because he is sure that he did "everything properly." This concern for his goodness stalled him before death until, after much torment, he was able to say, "It was all not the right thing, but that's no matter." At that point he hears someone nearby say, "It is finished." The words reverberate in his soul as, "Death is finished. It is no more." "Then he drew in a breath, stopped in the midst of a sigh, stretched out, and died."[10]

Tolstoy's story, unlike Kubler-Ross's description of the final stage of dying, concentrates on the patient's inner struggle with death. Tolstoy sees not just a withdrawal from the world but an intense struggle with ultimate questions —Why is this happening? Who have I been? How am I justified? Tolstoy's answers may not be our own, but what matters is that he recognizes the reality and intensity of the struggle. He maintains that we may reach a point before death where we stop defending what we have done or been. In that moment of self-surrender, caused in Ilych by hearing Christ's last words on the cross, we arrive at a point where we are able to give ourselves to death and to whatever lies beyond it. We live into the future, putting our trust in God and in what God has in store for us.

CONCLUSION

Faith bears many fruits. We have seen that it sends us into the world to live and to serve the neighbor in need. We have also seen that it changes the self's relation to itself. It allows us to live until we die, for it gives us assurance and courage beyond any force that seeks to destroy it. It enables us to accept what has been, to live with what is, and to embrace what is to come, even as death threatens to take all these things from us. That is the power of faith or, more precisely, that is the gift that we receive from a God who sustains, redeems, and recreates us in the midst of dying.

CHAPTER 8

CONCRETE INSTANCES OF FAITH

IN THIS FINAL CHAPTER, I WANT TO ILLUSTRATE how the different dimensions of faith manifest themselves in the lives of people who face the prospect of death. I propose to take an extended look at two different situations, one that occurred in the sixteenth century and one that happened in recent years. In the first situation the role of faith is up-front and obvious; in the second situation the role of faith is more intangible and hidden. Together the two situations give a concrete picture of the parameters of faith as it responds to death.

THE DEATH OF A DAUGHTER

On September 20, 1542, Martin Luther's thirteen-year-old daughter Magdalena died. The cause of death is not disclosed except to say that she died after a brief and painful illness. Luther was at her side. His wife Katie, who was in the throes of grief, was farther from the bed.

Magdalena's death was not peaceful, though Luther was sure that she died "confessing Christ." When she was "in the agony of death, [Luther] fell upon his knees before the bed and, weeping bitterly, prayed that God might save her if it be his will." "She gave up the ghost in the arms of her father."[1]

Luther did not try to hide his pain. Several days after Magdalena's death, he wrote to Justas Jonas, a friend and former dean of the theological faculty in Wittenberg: "Although I and my wife ought to do nothing but joyfully give thanks for such a felicitous passage and blessed end, . . . so great is the force of our love that we are unable to go on without sobs and groanings of heart, indeed without bearing in ourselves a mortal wound."[2] Luther was impatient with himself. "I am angry with myself that I am unable to rejoice from my heart and be thankful to God, although I do at times sing a little hymn and thank God."[3] Three years later Luther was still in grief: "It is astonishing how much the death of my Magdalena torments me, which I have not yet been able to forget."[4]

Our main concern in this tragedy is with the effect that Magdalena's death had on Luther's faith. Luther acknowledged the need to mourn. Three years earlier he had written to Catherine Metzler, a friend who in a period of eight months had lost both her husband and a son: "It is natural and right that you should grieve, especially for one who is of your own flesh and blood. For God has not created us to be without feeling or to be like stones or sticks, but it is his will that we should mourn and bewail our dead."[5] Luther usually attached an important qualification to this permission, especially after his own daughter's death. Mourning should be done in moderation or, as he says, it should be held in check. No doubt, Luther had in mind Paul's admonition to the Thessalonians that—given the promise of the resurrection—we should grieve but not "as others do who have no hope" (1 Thessalonians 4:13). Luther was concerned that the intensity of grief would not reflect negatively on the comfort of the Word.

Luther assigned an important role to suffering in general and to grief in particular. He maintained that "faith is born only on the brink of despair."[6] Given our persistent and deeply-rooted tendency to rely on ourselves, Luther believed that God must use radical means to increase, or even to sustain, our faith in and reliance upon God. Suffering, even unto death, is one of those means. And for Luther this harsh treatment is a manifestation of God's love for his children, and not a sign of God's displeasure and wrath. "There is perhaps no greater sign of God's parental concern than the care with which he designs the individual course of affliction for His children."[7] Thus, paradoxically, the tremendous challenges that God poses to the Christian's faith are the very means by which it is engendered and strengthened."[8]

So God must first take away before God can give. God must first empty before God can fill. This paradoxical realization addressed but did not take away Luther's grief. "The spirit is willing but the flesh is weak. I love her very much."[9] The poignancy of Luther's grief shows through, but it did not render him inconsolable, because his faith provided a measure of comfort. A month or two after Magdalena's death he found solace in the fact that she had died "confessing Christ," and he was consoled by the belief that his beloved daughter had gone to her Father in heaven.

In addressing friends and colleagues who had lost loved ones, Luther suggested other thoughts to provide comfort, all of which were practical or pastoral extensions of his faith in the gospel. To the widow of John Cellarius, he said that she should be comforted by the realization that her "sorrow is not the greatest experienced by the children of men. There are many who suffer and endure a hundred times as much."[10] In other circumstances, Luther adds to this thought a reference to some biblical character who endured great loss, like Abraham who was commanded to kill his own son or like

David who learned that his son Absalom intended to drive him out of his own kingdom.[11] If these thoughts do not comfort, then the realization that no sorrow, "no death can be compared with [the trials of the] innocent Son of God [who] suffered for us and for our salvation,"[12] should surely help.

Luther makes other suggestions. He consoles Ambrose Berndt, a former student at Wittenberg, with the thought that his wife died in childbirth, that is, "in the performance of her God-given duty and in the exercise of her proper calling."[13] He reminds the parents of John Knudsen that John "cheated the world and the devil"[14] by escaping "the perilous and evil times"[15] in which they still live. But mostly Luther tried to comfort, when appropriate, by reminding mourners that the deceased had died a good death. For example, regarding Thomas Zink's young son he said, "He fell asleep . . . decently and softly with such a fine testimony of his faith on his lips that we all marveled."[16]

Luther had great respect for the power of grief, partly because he had lost a seven-month-old daughter fourteen years before he lost Magdalena. In a letter to Conrad Cordatus, a pastor in Zwickau who lost a newly-baptized son, Luther begins by telling him that he should be comforted, because Christ wanted the child "with him rather than with you, for he is safer there than here," but he stops in midstream and says, "But all this is vain, a story that falls on deaf ears, when your grief is so new. I therefore yield to your sorrow."[17] Luther was right, but like Job's friends he could not leave it there. He had a message to convey, an assurance to give, and he proceeds to give it. "It is a good thing for you . . . to have had this kind of trial . . . so that you may learn in your own experience what is that power of the Word and of faith which is proved in these agonies."[18]

We may question some of Luther's pastoral practice. We do not think it is especially helpful to compare a person's grief with those who apparently suffered more or to remind a husband that his wife's death in childbirth was a fulfillment of a duty or to say to a grieving father that his son's death can teach him a lesson about the power of the Word. Luther did not sit on the mourner's bench with the mourner as long as he should have. Instead he believed that the mourner would find comfort in God's Word, and he was anxious to get to that Word as soon as possible, not as an incarnated truth in a concrete relationship but as a verbal or written announcement of God's mercy and comfort. For Luther, this was not an avoidance of grief as much as it was a firm conviction that in the face of death the individual's faith needed to be aroused or increased and that the only way to do that was by Word and Sacrament. Luther's "ministry to troubled souls" becomes a "ministry of the gospel,"[19] that is, a ministry of witnessing to God's grace and comfort as the only sure way to help the troubled soul live by and draw sustenance from "the Father of mercies and the God of all consolation" (2 Corinthians 1:3).

While we can grant the logic of Luther's reasoning, really the logic of his faith, his pastoral practice of bringing in the assurance of God as quickly as he can raises a serious question for us today. Is the Word of God an immediate answer to grief's, or death's, agonizing questions? In part our question is also Luther's question, because when he lost Magdalena he did not find God's Word of immediate help. He had to give his intense grief its due, whether he wanted to or not. But for us the question is more pressing, partly because we are much less theocentric than Luther was. When we read Luther's letters to the bereaved, for example, we find his quick references to God, and especially his firm conviction that God is at work in the loss, less than convincing or comforting.[20] With C. S. Lewis we experience the absence or even the judgment of God, or with Harold S. Kushner we experience the unfairness of our suffering or even the limited scope of God's power.

Our faith must take our reaction seriously, not by giving up on the Word but by approaching it in personal or pastoral relationships in a different, less direct way. To clarify, let me turn to a second situation, to a contemporary struggle with death.

THE "DEATH" OF A HUSBAND

Mr. D,[21] a thirty-three-year-old construction worker, seemed in good health. He enjoyed physical activity and was skilled with his hands. In his spare time, he repaired "things around the house" and felt fulfilled when he was working on cars.

Mr. D and his wife DD were married for twelve years when after much marital conflict DD moved out of the house and did not return for three months. The couple then went for marital counseling, but the conflict between them continued.

About a month after DD returned home, Mr. D and a few friends attended a sports event in Baltimore. The game was tense and exciting. Suddenly Mr. D collapsed, and when all efforts to revive him failed he was rushed to a local hospital. A CAT scan was taken and showed that Mr. D had an aneurysm in a cerebral artery, diminishing the supply of oxygen to the brain. The doctor scheduled surgery for the same day but later decided to postpone it for a day so Mr. D "could stabilize." When surgery was performed, it was considered successful, and the doctor predicted that Mr. D would begin to wake up in twenty-four to forty-eight hours and that the swelling of the brain from surgery would subside during the next week. Meanwhile, Mr. D rested comfortably on a respirator.

Mr. D did not wake up as predicted. Two weeks went by and still no response. Mr. D was moved from critical care to intensive care. His wife came to the hospital daily, and his parents were frequent visitors.

Time passed. Tests indicated that Mr. D had "extensive brain damage." Occasionally, he would yawn, open his eyes, and seem to smile, but the surgeons thought it was only "neurological activity," since they could not elicit any response from Mr. D. After a month and a half, the doctors raised the possibility of removing Mr. D from the respirator and asked the family to discuss it. They suggested to DD that it would be better to remove life support and allow Mr. D to die. To wait longer could mean that Mr. D's death would be drawn out and more difficult.

DD hoped for a miracle. A few of her church friends gathered outside of Mr. D's hospital room and prayed for healing. Mr. D showed no sign of improvement. In fact, he came down with a lung infection and seemed to be deteriorating fast. The hospital treated the infection, but the doctors still pressed for a decision about the respirator.

Reluctantly, DD consulted with her husband's parents and found herself arguing for the removal of life support. The parents were set against it, and DD decided to make an appointment with the pastor "to think things through." When she saw the pastor, she started talking about funeral arrangements, since she could see the "handwriting on the wall."

Several weeks pass. Mr. D remained in a coma. The parents seemed more open to pulling the plug, and after days of indecision a final decision was made. The plug was pulled, and Mr. D breathed on his own—a day, then a week, then a month. He opened his eyes temporarily, and DD took this as a ray of hope and asked the doctors to retest Mr. D. The tests confirmed extensive damage to the brain.

DD continued to visit Mr. D regularly. Mr. D was moved to a small room and given minimal care in the expectation that he could die anytime. One mid-week morning, DD entered Mr. D's room and greeted him as usual. Mr. D opened his eyes and returned the greeting. DD was shocked, but when Mr. D continued to respond over the next several days, she had him moved to a rehabilitation center that had a brain injury unit. He spent three to four months there and progressed from a wheel-chair to a walker. He was finally ready to go home, still suffering from short-term memory loss and impaired reasoning. In response to the pastor's request, several men from the congregation volunteered to take turns reading to Mr. D and playing checkers with him as part of his ongoing care. Eventually, Mr. D was able to walk with a cane and to carry on a normal conversation but with limited cognitive ability.

Over the next year and a half, DD reached a breaking point. Mr. D was belligerent and verbally abusive to the children. He sat passively in front of the TV all day and became almost totally dependent on DD. DD worked extra time to try to keep the family afloat, and finally she could not take it any longer. She filed for divorce, and Mr. D ended up living in a community care facility. He maintained sporadic contact with the children.

Mr. D's closeness to death is filled with bioethical issues, but our focus is on DD's faith as she struggles with the "loss" of her husband. Unlike Luther's situation, DD's situation has very few references to faith. Faith has become a private issue in our society, so even when it is an obvious consideration in any one situation it is seldom, if ever, discussed in any depth. We must look below the surface, then, to see how faith played a part in DD's struggle with impending death.

DD put her immediate trust in the doctors. For her, Mr. D's condition was not a religious problem but a medical problem, and she clung to the resources of medical science in order to obtain a correct diagnosis and a proper course of treatment. She was not disappointed. Surgery was performed on the problem, and the surgeon assured her that the operation was successful. She simply had to stand by and wait for Mr. D to wake up from the trauma. And when he did, she would be relieved of the guilt that her mother-in-law induced in her because she had separated from Mr. D and thereby had caused him untold tension.

DD, and the medical staff, waited, but Mr. D did not gain consciousness. By this time, DD's pastor was involved. His presence took DD from the day-to-day concerns of care and gave her permission to respond to the religious dimensions of her situation. The pastor was an assurance of God's presence, even an assurance that God was good and intended the best for Mr. D. DD believed this, and yet she did not believe it. She knew too many people who had looked to God for help, some of whom even had members of the congregation praying for them, but nothing much seemed to happen. Nevertheless, the pastor was comforting. His expression of concern and his unspoken but underlying confidence that God was there, assured her that she was not alone in her confusion and grief. And when the pastor prayed, he gave expression to her anxiety and asked that she be given strength to stand by with patience and hope. It was a blessing to have her needs lifted above the confines of the hospital room and placed before God.

Visits from friends and fellow church members were also a comfort. Some people tried to make the visit merely a social event, like they were just dropping in for a short time to pass the time of day. DD appreciated their thoughtfulness in coming, and she knew that their intention was to convey concern. But their uneasiness with Mr. D's comatose condition reminded her of the gravity of the situation. Other people were more at ease, especially if they had had a recent experience with significant illness or loss and had been comforted. If they resisted the temptation to tell of their experience in order to try to show that they could understand what DD was going through, they were often "able to console . . . with the consolation" that they themselves had received (2 Corinthians 1:4). It was not necessarily their words that conveyed comfort, but the confidence that they had that there was an answer, a light at the end of the tunnel. In either case, the care of fellow believers, whether expressed by card or visit, went a long way to enflesh, to make real the care of God, whether DD thought of it in those terms or not.

Over time DD's faith underwent significant change, more subtle than dramatic. In the beginning she wondered what God was trying to do. Sometimes when someone asked her how Mr. D was doing, she caught an angry undertone in her voice, like she was mad at God or something. As time went on and Mr. D got worse, she was surprised to find that the anger was gone and in its place was a passing recognition that she was desperate and needed help. She was unprepared for what she found herself doing when she made an appointment with the pastor to talk about unplugging the respirator. She talked instead about funeral arrangements. Had she come to the point where she could admit that Mr. D was dying and actually begin to make arrangements for it? The thought frightened her, but it was not devastating.

As DD sat many long hours at Mr. D's side, she had ample time to reflect on life and their marriage. When Mr. D was first hospitalized, she spent four days going between his room and the waiting room. After that she visited him daily, even though for awhile he was being kept in a coma in order to lessen the chance that his intracranial pressure (ICP) would rise. Over time DD noticed a marked change in Mr. D's body. Initially he was big and strong, and his face was peaceful as though he were in a deep sleep. Months later he had lost a lot of weight, his legs were thin and weak, and his face wrinkled and as though in pain. As DD observed the change, ironically Mr. D became more precious. She no longer took him for granted but began to think of him as a gift. She cherished the time with him, even though the hours seemed endless and he showed no sign of responding. Occasionally, she caught herself thinking, "Gee, I'm beginning to see Mr. D as God must see him—as a creature of great value whatever his outward appearance."

DD looked forward to Sundays when she could attend services at her church. At first the pastor seemed surprised to see her, because other parishioners who were going through hard times had found the sudden attention and hurried expressions of concern difficult to take. But DD needed the support of her friends and the ritual of a worshiping community. The elements of the worship—the Invocation with its call to worship, the Kyrie with its theme of peace, the sermon with its proclamation of God-at-work, the prayers with their petitions for those in need, the Benediction with its parting words of blessing and protection—all provided a kind of comfort. There were times, of course, when people would say the wrong thing. There were times when either DD was "not with it" or the Word of God was not helpful. But mostly DD was hearing the Word as she had not heard it before, and she was clinging to the promises of God like they were a life raft on a turbulent sea. It was most difficult for her to "pass the peace," because as friends embraced her and whispered, "The peace of the Lord be with you always," she fought back tears and hung on longer than she should.

DD's struggle with faith and death came to a climax when the doctors kept pushing her to take Mr. D off the respirator. For the doctors it was the clinical thing to do. For DD it was giving up a life. Initially she resisted, but gradually, sadly she saw "the handwriting on the wall." She was ready, but Mr. D's parents weren't. Several weeks went by, and the day of decision arrived. Taking a deep breath she said to herself, "God, I put his life into your hands." A great load was taken off of her shoulders. The plug was pulled, and Mr. D breathed on his own. She was surprised and pleased. She was utterly taken aback when one morning her husband opened his eyes and said, "Hi."

Comparing faith as it was manifested in the case of Luther and of DD, we are inclined to say that Luther's direct witness to the Word would not be very effective in this day. We live in a time when references to religious beliefs in the midst of a major crisis are easily labeled religious platitudes and are not seen as especially effective in conveying God's presence or comfort. We might find DD's case more realistic. Her faith does not show, and yet it seems to be a genuine and living force as death lurks nearby. Our reaction to both situations needs to be refined further.

In our book, *Preaching God's Compassion,*[22] Robert Hughes and I maintained that there are practical differences between preaching and pastoral care and that the pastor needs to witness to the gospel in different ways in each form of ministry. In preaching, the pastor can proclaim the message of God directly, "whether or not the listener is in an existential position to affirm or accept it, [for] preaching is the community of faith declaring its faith and thereby inviting the troubled parishioner to live by the promise."[23] If the listener cannot believe it or live by it because he or she is immersed in grief or some other struggle, still that person may gain some comfort from it, either immediately or in retrospect, because it represents the community's ray of light in the midst of personal darkness. Pastoral care often requires a different approach. In personal relationships with the pastor or with friends, the grieving parishioner needs to be listened to, needs to be able to articulate his or her struggle with death and to have it addressed by incarnate, relational care, and not so much by quick verbal assurances.

Luther was too much the preacher. He was right in maintaining that the gospel should inform his pastoral care, but he was wrong in assuming that verbal proclamation of the gospel was appropriate for both pulpit and pastoral relationship.

DD raises her own issues related to faith. She is a this-worldly person more than she is an other-worldly person, and, like most people who are in a crisis, she is preoccupied with immediate concerns, namely the course of Mr. D's illness, the routine of the hospital, the nurses' care of Mr. D, the restlessness of Mr. D's roommate, the children at home, etc. She seldom, if ever, thought of her situation in terms of faith. She needed someone like the pastor to slow her down and to give her permission to deal with issues of faith. Even then her struggle might be addressed in a perfunctory way, and she might emerge from the whole experience unaware of the impact that it has had on her spiritual life. This is certainly true if she or her friends or her pastor are inclined to deal with the situation by denying the possibility or the presence of death.

There is a principle in psychotherapy that is relevant here. My version of this Freudian insight is something like this: An idea or a feeling is not fully potentiated until it is recognized and articulated. We have an example of this principle in the student who experienced an oceanic insight in my office.[24] He had been struggling with a problem for nearly an hour and had not been able to clarify it or to experience it. Suddenly it became clear to him, and in that moment it took on a healing power that it did not have before.

In the same way, a faith struggle that is not acknowledged or articulated is left in a relatively unfulfilled state.

It does not become an occasion of acute awareness or an occasion of growth. Nevertheless, all is not necessarily lost. The situation itself can be used by the Holy Spirit to grab our attention and encourage us to attend to its implications for our faith. DD experienced this "breaking in" at several points—when the pastor prayed in the hospital room, when DD found herself talking about funeral arrangements, and when she was able to let go and turn Mr. D over to God. She could have also experienced a "breaking in" if at the right time the pastor, or a fellow believer, had invited her to reflect on and to share how her faith was faring under the circumstances.

Luther and DD represent two different manifestations of faith. In the end one is not necessarily better than the other. What is important is that the person is empowered to grasp onto God, for as we have seen faith is a matter of life and death. It anchors our life in an abiding presence even as we approach the destruction of death. It is a leap beyond all human resources, a leap without which we cannot live fully the life we have left.

THE LEAP OF FAITH

To place our faith in someone or something beyond the self is to admit that we are not self-sufficient, that we need help from the outside. The question is, "How radical is our admission?" The Apostle Paul requires an unconditional admission, an acknowledgment that we must rely totally on God for care, grace, and renewal. In other words, living by faith in Paul's sense knocks all other props out from under us. No earthly things can give us final security; no self-generated works can assure us of God's favor. Faith is truly a leap, a radical living out of the first commandment, "You shall have no other gods before me" (Deuteronomy 5:7).

Faith in Paul's sense is also a recognition that it is a gift, an empowerment from God that makes it possible for an otherwise self-reliant creature to look beyond the self for forgiveness and fulfillment. Our faith is a confession that we cannot by our own "reason or strength believe in Jesus Christ. . . . or come to Him."[25]

In this study, I have focused on the human side of faith, on how it is a response to God's initiative. We have not cited anyone who has lived up to Paul's understanding of faith, not even Luther or Paul himself. And we have not laid out a definite progression of faith as though our faith proceeds by linear steps from a simple faith to a refined one. Instead we have maintained with Luther that faith is a paradoxical anomaly where both faith and doubt exist side-by-side, even as one grows in faith. Growth in faith, then, means that ideally we are able increasingly to cast ourselves on God's Word in the midst of doubt and despair. In any case, faith, even a refined faith, does not produce a super-Christian, one who relies on God in any circumstances. At best, we are always sinners on the way to becoming believers, which means that we are estranged from God but always on the way to becoming, not saints, but vessels of imputed righteousness.[26]

Our study has brought faith into extended conversation with death. In one sense, death stands at the end of our lives, but in another sense—in a Pauline sense—it stands at the center of our lives. As the wages of sin, or even as an indelible boundary of life, death is a dark shadow that casts its image on everything we are and do. We build larger barns to accommodate our bumper crop and then receive the message, "Fool! This very night your soul is being demanded of you" (Luke 12:20). We arrive at a moment of tranquility after much turmoil, and the next moment we are drawn into war with our neighbor. We become reconciled to our estranged son or daughter, and then he or she is killed in an automobile accident. Death in one form or another is an omnipresent part of life.

Death is also the ultimate test of our faith. It leaves nothing undisturbed, including our untested faith. Faith under fire can either regress or recover. If it regresses, it grabs onto former formulations of comfort and may be ill-prepared for the next onslaught. If it recovers, hopefully it will also be refined, emerging with a deeper understanding of God's way and clinging ever more zealously to God's Word. It is the clinging that makes faith salutary, for it is a clinging to God's grace and comfort. In the face of death, only an ultimate Power can take away the sting of death, only the Source of life can heal and revive our broken spirit.

I began this study by maintaining that there is a distinction to be made between death as a psychological struggle and death as a faith struggle. I also maintained that the church, both pastors and laypersons, have often focused on the former to the neglect of the latter. I have tried to correct this omission by taking an extended look at faith and its various dimensions as it confronts death. The discussion has ranged from the frailty of faith to the fruits of faith as seen from a Christian, especially from a Pauline, perspective. I have concluded what Christians down through the ages have concluded—that faith is a dynamic and essential resource in our struggle with death.

Our preoccupation with death as a struggle of faith rather than as a struggle of grief may imply that there is no relation between them. On the contrary, I contend that while they may represent two different approaches to death, they are not really two separate struggles. In life as we live it, there is no hard line between a believer's faith and a believer's grief. Thus as I discussed the various dimensions of faith in this book, I also addressed the various dimensions or dynamics of grief. For example, in my discussion of the foolishness of faith (chapter 4), I dealt with the mourner's struggle with hope and hopelessness, with meaning and meaninglessness. Or in my discussion of the tenacity of faith (chapter 5), I dealt with the mourner's struggle with loneliness and separation and, more indirectly, with anger. Or again in my discussion of the assurances of faith (chapter 6), I dealt with the mourner's struggle with abandonment and guilt. And throughout the book we returned constantly to a basic component of grief, namely, sadness and despair.[27]

Faith's relation to grief goes deeper than dealing with the emotional components of grief, however valid and necessary that is. Faith actually delivers us to grief or, to put it more cautiously, it empowers us to grieve. Instead of prompting us to deny our sorrow or to pretend that we have an immediate answer to grief, faith gives us the courage to grieve. It enables us to relate to death for what it is—a dreadful and formidable enemy. In this sense, faith undermines our popular misuse of it. In common Christian parlance, we often imply that if a person has enough faith, he or she should not grieve. We ascribe to faith a magical power that it does not have, and therefore we invite the mourner, actually we may push the mourner, to minimize his or her grief and to substitute for it a ready-mix comfort. The Word of God is a comfort, but it was never meant to be an instant and easy solution to an agonizing loss.

If faith delivers us to grief, it also empowers us to go through grief. It puts us in touch with God's care. It assures us that God is with us in our suffering. It gives us the courage to walk "through the darkest valley" and fear no evil (Psalm 23:4), for we live and die in the hope that "as Christ was raised from the dead. . . . We too might walk in newness of life" (Romans 6:4).

$\mathcal{N}$OTES

INTRODUCTION

1. Robert E. Neale, *The Art of Dying* (New York: Harper & Row, 1973).
2. Margaretta K. Bowers, et al., *Counseling the Dying* (New York: Thomas Nelson & Sons, 1964).
3. Kurt Eissler, *The Psychiatrist and the Dying Patient* (New York: International Universities Press, 1955).
4. Paul Irion, *Hospice and Ministry* (Nashville: Abingdon, 1988).
5. LeRoy Aden, David G. Benner, and J. Harold Ellens, eds, *Christian Perspectives on Human Development* (Grand Rapids, Mich.: Baker Book House, 1992), chapter 1, 19-33.
6. James W. Fowler, *Stages of Faith: The Psychology of Human Development and the Quest for Meaning* (New York: Harper & Row, 1981).
7. Erich Lindemann, "Symptomatology and Management of Acute Grief," *Pastoral Psychology,* XIV (September, 1963), 8-18.

CHAPTER 1

1. C. S. Lewis, *A Grief Observed* (New York: Seabury, 1963), 25.
2. *Ibid.,* 44.
3. Harold S. Kushner, *When Bad Things Happen to Good People* (New York: Schocken, 1981), 2-3.
4. Robert Kolb and Timothy J. Wengert, eds., *The Book of Concord* (Minneapolis: Fortress Press, 2000), 354.
5. Lewis, *A Grief Observed*, 31.
6. *Ibid.,* 15.
7. *Ibid.,* 33.
8. *Ibid.,* 35.
9. Kushner, *When Bad Things Happen to Good People,* 12-13.
10. *Ibid.,* 14.
11. *Ibid.,* 17.
12. *Ibid.,* 37.
13. *Ibid.,* 55.
14. *Ibid.,* 58.
15. *Ibid.,* 81.
16. *Ibid.,* 44.

17. Carl R. Rogers, *On Becoming a Person: A Therapist's View of Psychotherapy* (Boston: Houghton Mifflin, 1961).
18. For Rogers' elaboration of this point, see Carl R. Rogers, *On Becoming a Person: A Therapist's View of Psychotherapy* (Boston: Houghton Mifflin, 1961), 35-36; 350-351.
19. William Shakespeare, "The Tragedy of Hamlet," *Five Tragedies* (Boston: D. C. Heath and Company, 1917), 63.

CHAPTER 2

1. The frailty of faith may appear after the funeral, and not be evident when one is preoccupied with taking care of the dying person.
2. C. S. Lewis, *A Grief Observed* (New York: Seabury, 1963), 4-5.
3. Paul Tillich, *Systematic Theology* (Chicago: University of Chicago Press, 1951), I, 170.
4. C. W. Wahl, "The Fear of Death," in Herman Feifel, ed., *The Meaning of Death* (New York: McGraw-Hill Book, 1959), 25.
5. Arthur C. McGill, *Death and Life: An American Theology* (Philadelphia: Fortress Press, 1987), 11.
6. *Ibid.*
7. Leo Tolstoy, *The Death of Ivan Ilych and Other Stories* (New York: New American Library of World Literature, 1960), 131.
8. *Ibid.,* 134.
9. *Ibid.,* 131f.
10. Andras Angyal, *Neurosis & Treatment: A Holistic Theory.* Edited by E. Hanfmann and R. M. Jones. (New York: John Wiley & Sons, 1965), 63f.
11. Hendrik M. Ruitenbeek, ed., *Death: Interpretations* (New York: Dell Publishing Co., 1969), chapter 2, 19-38.
12. *Ibid.,* 22.
13. *Ibid.,* 36.
14. See Lloyd R. Bailey, Sr., *Biblical Perspectives on Death* (Philadelphia: Fortress Press, 1979), 104.
15. Tolstoy, *The Death of Ivan Ilych and Other Stories,* 130.
16. Oscar Cullmann, "Immortality of the Soul or Resurrection of the Dead," in Krister Stendahl, *Immortality and Resurrection* (New York: Macmillan Co., 1965), 12-20.
17. *Ibid.,* 17.
18. *Ibid.*

CHAPTER 3

1. Sigmund Freud, *Collected Papers.* Edited by Ernest Jones. (London: Hogarth Press, 1956), IV, 305.
2. Ernest Becker, *The Denial of Death* (New York: Free Press, 1973).
3. *Ibid.,* 5.
4. Robert J. Lifton, *Death in Life* (New York: Random House, 1968).
5. Elisabeth Kubler-Ross, *On Death and Dying* (London: Macmillan Company, 1969).
6. Douglas John Hall, *God and Human Suffering: An Exercise in the Theology of the Cross* (Minneapolis: Augsburg, 1986), 43-47.

7. William James, *The Varieties of Religious Experience: A Study in Human Nature* (New York: Random House, 1902), 79.
8. For a helpful description of the three stages, see Perry D. LeFevre, *The Prayers of Kierkegaard* (Chicago: University of Chicago Press, 1956), 150-166.
9. Libuse Lukas Miller, *In Search of the Self: The Individual in the Thought of Kierkegaard* (Philadelphia: Muhlenberg Press, 1962).
10. The discussion of busyness is taken from my article "A Look at the Other Side of the Holidays" in *The Torch*, vol. 74 (Fall, 2000), 22-23.
11. Robert J. Lifton, "The Sense of Immortality: On Death and the Continuity of Life" in Herman Feifel, *New Meanings of Death*, (New York: McGraw-Hill Book, 1977), 274-290.
12. Helmut Thielicke, *Death and Life* (Philadelphia: Fortress, 1970), 196.
13. *Ibid.,* 22.

CHAPTER 4

1. I use the terms "folly" and "foolishness" in Paul's sense to refer to something that does not make sense to the rational mind, something that seems incredulous or even ludicrous. Paul says that the gospel is foolishness to the Gentiles. I am saying that faith, because it is faith in this gospel, can also seem irrational and foolish.
2. See Walther von Loewenich, *Luther's Theology of the Cross*, trans. Herbert I. A. Bouman (Minneapolis: Augsburg Publishing House, 1976).
3. Oscar Cullmann, "Immortality of the Soul or Resurrection of the Dead," in Krister Stendahl, *Immortality and Resurrection* (New York: Macmillan Company, 1965), 21.
4. *Lutheran Book of Worship* (Minneapolis: Augsburg; Philadelphia: Board of Publication, Lutheran Church in America, 1978), 70.
5. Victor Paul Furnish, *Theology and Ethics in Paul* (Nashville: Abingdon Press, 1963), 174.
6. *Lutheran Book of Worship,* Hymn #228.
7. C. K. Barrett, *The Second Epistle to the Corinthians* (New York: Harper & Row, 1973), 67.
8. Elisabeth Kubler-Ross, *On Death and Dying* (London: Macmillan Company, 1969), 129.
9. *The Interpreter's Dictionary of the Bible,* vol. 2 (Nashville: Abingdon, 1962), 641.
10. *Lutheran Book of Worship,* Hymn #294.
11. See C. S. Lewis, *A Grief Observed* (New York: Seabury, 1963), 78.

CHAPTER 5

1. Elisabeth Kubler-Ross, *On Death and Dying* (London: Macmillan Company, 1969), 106f.
2. *Ibid.,* 107.
3. *Ibid.*
4. *Ibid.,* 110.
5. See Ernest Becker, *The Denial of Death* (New York: Free Press, 1973).
6. Miss C was a counselee of mine. She died several years ago—destitute and alone.
7. Mrs. M is a former parishioner of a seminary student on a field education

placement. The student wrote up his contact with Mrs. M and shared the story with me. Mrs. M died several years ago.

CHAPTER 6

1. Miss J's story is taken from a series of letters that she wrote to a theologian/ friend. The theologian gave me some of the letters, because he sought my professional advice as a professor of pastoral care. Miss J died in the 1990s.
2. Robert Kolb and Timothy J. Wengert, eds., *The Book of Concord* (Minneapolis: Fortress Press, 2000), 354-356.
3. LeRoy H. Aden and Robert G. Hughes, *Preaching God's Compassion: Comforting Those Who Suffer* (Minneapolis: Fortress Press, 2002), 2-6. Some of the wording in this paragraph is taken from that earlier book.
4. Kolb and Wengert, *The Book of Concord,* 354.
5. LeRoy Aden, David G. Benner, and J. Harold Ellens, eds., *Christian Perspectives on Human Development* (Grand Rapids: Baker Book House, 1992), 91-92.
6. *Ibid.*
7. Kolb and Wengert, *The Book of Concord,* 319.
8. Philipp Melanchton, Martin Luther's colleague, described the Holy Spirit as *agitatio,* God in constant action.
9. Dietrich Bonhoeffer, *Letters and Papers from Prison* (New York: Macmillan Company, 1953), 14.
10. Kolb and Wengert, *The Book of Concord,* 355.
11. See Heiko A. Oberman, *Luther: Man between God and the Devil.* Trans. Eileen Welliser-Schwarzbart. (New Haven: Yale University Press, 1989), especially 320-324 (Luther's deathbed experience).

CHAPTER 7

1. Paul Althaus, *The Theology of Martin Luther.* Trans. Robert C. Schultz. (Philadelphia: Fortress Press, 1963), 246.
2. Erik H. Erikson, *Identity and the Life Cycle* (New York: International Universities Press, Inc., 1959), 98.
3. Nicholas Wolterstorff, *Lament for a Son* (Grand Rapids: Eerdmans, 1987). See also LeRoy H. Aden and Robert G. Hughes, *Preaching God's Compassion: Comforting Those Who Suffer* (Minneapolis: Fortress Press, 2002), 60-62.
4. Karen Horney, *Neurosis and Human Growth: The Struggle toward Self-Realization* (New York: Norton, 1950), 68. For a summary of Horney's theory of personality, see LeRoy H. Aden and Robert G. Hughes, *Preaching God's Compassion: Comforting Those Who Suffer* (Minneapolis: Fortress Press, 2002), 127-129.
5. *Ibid.,* 68.
6. *Ibid.,* 65.
7. Freud recognized the existence of a death instinct in us. As we have seen, the Old Testament believed that death was a natural culmination, if not a fulfillment, of life. These two views are not equivalent, but together they recognize that death is not foreign to our physiological and psychological existence.
8. Elisabeth Kubler-Ross, *On Death and Dying* (London: Macmillan Company, 1969), 100.

9. Leo Tolstoy, *The Death of Ivan Ilych and Other Stories* (New York: The New American Library of World Literature, 1969).

10. *Ibid.,* 156.

CHAPTER 8

1. *Luther: Letters of Spiritual Counsel*, ed. and trans. Theodore G. Tappert (Philadelphia: Westminster, 1945), 51.

2. Martin Luther, *Werke,* Kritische Gesamtausgabe (Weimar: Hermann Boehlaus Nachfolger, 1912), Br 10, Nr. 3794, 21. See also Jane E. Strohl, "Luther and the Word of Consolation" in *The Lutheran Theological Seminary Bulletin* (Winter 1987), Vol. 67, No. 1, 29.

3. *Luther: Letters of Spiritual Counsel,* 50f.

4. Luther, *Werke,* Br. 11 Nr. 4122, 9.

5. *Luther: Letters of Spiritual Counsel,* 72.

6. Jane E. Strohl, "Luther and the Word of Consolation" in *The Lutheran Theological Seminary Bulletin* (Winter 1987), Vol. 67, No. 1, 26.

7. *Ibid.*

8. *Ibid.*

9. *Luther: Letters of Spiritual Counsel,* 50.

10. *Ibid.,* 74.

11. *Ibid.,* 68.

12. *Ibid.,* 74.

13. *Ibid.,* 63.

14. *Ibid.,* 62.

15. *Ibid.,* 73.

16. *Ibid.,* 65.

17. *Ibid.,* 60.

18. *Ibid.*

19. *Ibid.,* 15.

20. In Luther's address to those who were bereaved, he often recognized the power or necessity of grief, e.g., in his sermon at the funeral of his prince, Duke John of Saxony. See *Luther's Works,* Vol. 51: *Sermons I.* John W. Doberstein, ed. (Philadelphia: Muhlenberg Press, 1959), 231-243.

21. The story of Mr. D and DD is a compilation of a number of similar situations.

22. LeRoy H. Aden and Robert G. Hughes, *Preaching God's Compassion: Comforting Those Who Suffer* (Minneapolis: Fortress Press, 2002).

23. *Ibid.,* 47.

24. See chapter 4, 61.

25. Robert Kolb and Timothy J. Wengert, eds., *The Book of Concord* (Minneapolis: Fortress Press, 2000), 355.

26. One of Luther's favorite Bible texts was that of the father of a possessed child who, when Jesus demanded faith for healing, exclaimed, "I believe; help my unbelief!" See Mark 9:24.

27. For an extended discussion of the dynamics of grief, see Kenneth R. Mitchell and Herbert Anderson, *All Our Losses, All Our Griefs: Resources for Pastoral Care* (Philadelphia: Westminster Press, 1983), chapter 4.